Empowerment
for a
New
Golden
Age

Mohammad Afzal Janjua

بسم الله الرحمن الرحيم

"Indeed
God does not change
the condition of a people
till they change their
state of mind."
(Qur'an 13:11)

INSPIRATION AND DEDICATION

Empowerment for a New Golden Age is the result of two exceptional learning opportunities; the first, in 1980-1982, with Shaykh Fadhlalla Haeri at Bayt-ud-Din - a Sufi retreat, located near San Antonio, Texas. And the other, from 2005 thru 2011, with Dr. Abdullah Gilani at IMAN, Los Angeles, California. Both of these experiences, for me, highlighted vital significance of always approaching the Qur'an afresh, with an open and inquisitive mind.

Mohammad Afzal Janjua

Houston, Texas

June, 2014

Empowerment for a New Golden Age

CONTENTS

Acknowledgments

A Note for the Readers   1

Chapter 1   Prelude   5

Chapter 2   Path to Success   17

Chapter 3   About the Path   33

Chapter 4   A God Willed Mission   67

Chapter 5   Gone Astray!   83

Chapter 6   An Eternal Message   111

Chapter 7   Retracing the Path   129

Chapter 8   A New Golden Age   151

Online Resources   155

About the Author   156

ACKNOWLEDGMENTS

I would like to thank Arzoo, Nadia, Sophia and Fatima who encouraged me to continue with this rather long protracted project. And, Noor and Hamza who kept me focused on putting together this book. I pray that Allah rewards all of them immensely for their patience, generosity, advice and priceless smiles.

A NOTE FOR THE READERS

This book, *Empowerment for a New Golden Age* - highlights the path that led to an era of advancement of knowledge, science, creativity, innovation, discovery and enlightenment; a period lasting for nearly a millennium in which ethnic and religious diversity was not only tolerated but was celebrated as a manifestation of the divine will, an epoch known as the *Islamic Golden Age*.

The book also identifies the factors that set into motion a process of decline of this epoch. And, it proposes a strategy for *empowerment*, enabling those who will heed, to retrace the highlighted path and to shape a *New Golden Age*.

It is obvious that when a community desires that it be recognized as an educated society - it undertakes establishment of necessary systems and institutions that enable its members to uplift their individual educational levels thus resulting in a collectively enlightened and educated society. Similarly, the shaping of a new golden age entails a collective sense of purpose, conscious commitment and transformation of mind set both at collective as well as individual level.

In order to facilitate pursuit of the proposed strategy for shaping of a new golden age, a separate publication titled "*Empowerment Guide for a New Golden Age - **Companion Workbook***" is being made available to be used at an individual level. This companion workbook is designed to provide a systematic approach for retracing the   path as highlighted in this book.

Please note that at several places English rendition of verses of the Qur'an have been quoted in this book. Generally these renditions are taken from "***The Message of The Qur'an***" *by* ***Muhammad Asad***. Whenever an alternative source is cited instead, in such case name of the translator is appended to the textual reference (Chapter : Verse) listed in the footnotes. The alternative translations, have typically, been taken either from "***The Meaning of the Glorious Koran***" *by* ***Marmaduke Pickthall*** or from "***The Meaning of The Holy Qur'an – Ammana***

published edition with Revised translation" by Abdullah Yusuf Ali.

Selection of *"The Message of The Qur'an by Muhammad Asad"* as a primary source in this book is due mainly to its more contemporary style of the English language. And also, the fact that Asad's rendition benefits from a vast amount of reference material, spanning centuries of related scholarly works, all of it identified and listed through the explanatory notes - which are numerous and informative, often providing reasoning for different viewpoints.

In some chapters (Surahs) of the Qur'an the numbers assigned to verses (Ayats) may vary by one or two, either way, due to slight variations in numbering method employed by various translators.

It is suggested that multiple English language renditions, along with the original Arabic text, of the herein quoted Qur'anic references, be consulted, in real-time mode, while reading this book. Scores of internet websites, each hosting

A Note for the Readers

multiple English renditions of the divine writ can be a useful resource for this purpose.

As a <u>special note</u>: the readers must keep in mind that it is customary for Muslims to voice the phrase "*Alayhe-Salaamm*" after the name of all prophets. The phrase means "peace be upon him" and it is generally depicted in writings either as (*AS*) or simply abbreviated as '*pbuh*'. Therefore, it is requested that Muslims should follow this custom when a prophet's name is read in this book.

Chapter One

Prelude

❖ *"ARE YOU NOT aware that God has made subservient to you all that is in the heavens and all that is on earth, and has lavished upon you His blessings, both outward and inward?"* [1]

On September 26, 2001, in a meeting of Global Corporate Leaders held in Minneapolis, Minnesota where the conference theme was *"Technology Business and Our Way of Life: What Next?"*, Ms. Carly Fiorina in her capacity as Chief Executive Officer of Hewlett-Packard, a leading multinational information technology company,

---

[1] [Qur'an 31:20]

delivered an informative lecture titled *"What does our future demand of leaders today?"*. She concluded her enlightening lecture[2] by sharing a story with the audience, in these words:

"I'll end by telling a story.

There was once a civilization that was the greatest in the world.

It was able to create a continental super-state that stretched from ocean to ocean and from northern climes to tropics and deserts. Within its dominion lived hundreds of millions of people, of different creeds and ethnic origins.

One of its languages became the universal language of much of the world, the bridge between the peoples of a hundred lands. Its armies were made up of people of many nationalities, and its military protection allowed a degree of peace and prosperity that had never been known. The reach of this civilization's commerce

---

[2] Carly Fiorina's complete speech can be viewed at:
"www.hp.com/hpinfo/execteam/speeches/fiorina/minnesota01.html"

extended from Latin America to China, and everywhere in between.

And this civilization was driven more than anything, by invention. Its architects designed buildings that defied gravity. Its mathematicians created the algebra and algorithms that would enable the building of computers, and the creation of encryption. Its doctors examined the human body, and found new cures for disease. Its astronomers looked into the heavens, named the stars, and paved the way for space travel and exploration.

Its writers created thousands of stories. Stories of courage, romance and magic. Its poets wrote of love, when others before them were too steeped in fear to think of such things.

When other nations were afraid of ideas, this civilization thrived on them, and kept them alive. When censors threatened to wipe out knowledge from past civilizations, this civilization kept the knowledge alive, and passed it on to others.

While modern Western civilization shares many of these traits, the civilization I'm talking about was the Islamic world from the year 800 to 1600, which included the Ottoman Empire and the courts of Baghdad, Damascus and Cairo, and enlightened rulers like Suleiman the Magnificent.

Although we are often unaware of our indebtedness to this other civilization, its gifts are very much a part of our heritage. The technology industry would not exist without the contributions of Arab mathematicians. Sufi poet-philosophers like Rumi challenged our notions of self and truth. Leaders like Suleiman contributed to our notions of tolerance and civic leadership.

And perhaps we can learn a lesson from his example: It was leadership based on meritocracy, not inheritance. It was leadership that harnessed the full capabilities of a very diverse population that included Christianity, Islamic, and Jewish traditions.

This kind of enlightened leadership — leadership that nurtured culture, sustainability, diversity and courage — led to 800 years of invention and prosperity."

Fiorina closed her lecture by saying: *"In dark and serious times like this, we must affirm our commitment to building societies and institutions that aspire to this kind of greatness. More than ever, we must focus on the importance of leadership – bold acts of leadership and decidedly personal acts of leadership.*

With that, I'd like to open up the conversation and see what we, collectively, believe about the role of leadership."

And now a brief mention of another summit, under the auspices of the *World Islamic Economic Forum Foundation,* which was held on May 28, 2007 at Kuala Lumpur, Malaysia. In this meeting Prime Minister Abdullah Ahmad Badawi[3] noted that the fifty-seven members of the Organization of the Islamic Conference (OIC)

---

[3] Prime Minister of Malaysia from 2003 to 2009

accounted for only five percent of the world's gross domestic product in 2005 despite comprising twenty-one percent of the global population. And later in the same assembly Malaysia, Indonesia, Kuwait, the United Arab Emirates and Pakistan brought to attention of the audience that many of the 1.6 billion Muslims globally rank among the world's poorest people. The five nations challenged Islamic countries to work together to create a *New Golden Age* to liberate Muslims from poverty, conflict and extremism.[4]

Years later, far from taking on the challenge of working together to create a *New Golden Age*, the Muslim societies remain mired in stagnation and decay; unremitting poverty, low standards of literacy, abysmal attention to human rights, widening gap between haves and have-nots, astounding inequalities in income and wealth, gender imparity and abuse, sectarian strife, ethnic adversities, corrupt governments, whimsical approach to justice, repressive officialdoms and *Jahiliyya*[5] cloaked as

---

[4] http://www.chinapost.com.tw/international/110891.htm
[5] State of a mindset commonly referring to pre-Islamic ignorance

religious conservatism - are some of the festering problems plaguing the Muslim Ummah[6] today.

An objective analysis of the two scenarios presented in the aforementioned meetings; that of the Global Corporate Leaders in Minneapolis and the World Islamic Economic Forum in Kuala Lumpur, reveals two distinctly different mindsets; the former that radiated through the story of the *Greatest Civilization* as narrated by Fiorina – this mindset was driven by innovation, creativity, discovery and faith; and the latter depicting today's Muslim Ummah - a specter of pathetic incompetence - it finds solace in conformity, imitation, ignorance and skepticism, it is adrift rudderless on the world stage. This latter mindset - the one resigned to subservience and subjugation – forgetful of the past unlike that of its ancestors and unmindful of its future rather uncaring of the successors, it seems that the inspiration that ignited fashioning of the world's greatest civilization,

---

[6] **Ummah** is an Arabic word meaning "nation" or "community". Without a qualifier, it is commonly used to mean the collective community of Islamic peoples.

over fourteen centuries ago, has completely vanished or been permanently lost.

The challenge *"to create a New Golden Age"*, posed at the World Islamic Economic Forum[7], targeted reviving the *Greatest Civilization* - the focus of Fiorina's story. And even though this exact challenge is presented often, yet there is never a real actionable plan or program proposed for actualization of this rhetoric. The oft repeated desire to "work together" also remains unfulfilled, as without a clear idea of how and what it is that these peoples are supposed to "work together" for, the call to action remains but only an empty rhetoric.

In recent times, electronic media, especially internet and television, have acquired particularly important roles in mass education. A program titled *"Rick Steves' Andalucia"*[8] that featured on public television in the United States and which can also be viewed through the internet, provides visual glimpse of some of

---

[7] The meeting made mention of on page 7, which was held on May 28, 2007 at Kuala Lumpur,

[8] www.ricksteves.com/tvr/pledge/andalucia/andalucia_details.htm

the cities that were once brilliant examples of the civilization that was the focus of Fiorina's story.

In one such episode for example, the camera shows the viewers a glimpse of the exquisitely charming city of Córdoba, its art, culture and architecture. As the program host and the tour guide walk through narrow flower-bedecked lanes that invite exploration, fresh little streets, the narrowness and white-washed walls of which provide natural air-conditioning - a feeling of coolness - they marvel at the ingenuity, innovation and the architecture as simply brilliant.

As the presenters stroll through the city, the streets and landmarks, they recall to mind the magical *Al Andalus*[9], with its enlightened culture and the exquisite city of Córdoba. One can vividly picture the grandeur of this great civilization of the *Islamic Golden Age*, which boasted great achievements in economy, arts, philosophy, literature, mathematics, science,

---

[9] *Refers to Muslim ruled Iberian Peninsula - between 711 and 1492. Though Al Andalus' boundaries kept changing, overall it comprised of the parts of what is today Spain, Portugal, Gibraltar and France.*

architecture and technology as its power and influence steadily grew through flourishing trade across Asia, Europe and Africa.

They, the presenters defined Córdoba of the 10th century, as inarguably Europe's greatest city - a cultural capital; it had probably more than ten times the population of Paris. Imagine a city of over a millennium ago; with paved streets, lit at night by oil lamps, piped in running water, hundreds of mosques, palaces, and public baths. A city of poets and scholars - it coined the term *La Convivencia* ("the Coexistence") - depicting not only mutual respect and tolerance but a remarkable spirit of solidarity among all its inhabitants of different religious traditions: Muslims, Christians and Jews.

The tour guide goes on to highlight the fact that even though people belonging to three different religions inhabited the city - it was in fact one integrated culture as they all spoke the same language - Arabic, they cooked the same foods and they wore the same clothes.

In addition to Cordoba, several other cities, such as Baghdad and Bukhara, Cairo and

Kostantiniyye[10], Fez and Samarkand, Isfahan and Damascus, to name but just a few of the sophisticated metropolises that featured beautiful architecture, exquisite gardens, public bath houses, centers of learning, libraries, hospitals, and a rich vibrant all inclusive culture that typified the *Islamic Golden age*.

In the modern times when bigotry, racism and intolerance is on the rise in the west, and spewing of hate against Islam has in fact become an industry, the humankind more than ever, needs to reacquaint itself with the mindset that shaped a millennium long practice of coexistence and respect for religious and ethnic diversity as modeled by *Al Andalus* and typified by the term *La Convivencia*.

A distressed state of the prevailing global financial systems, rapidly depleting state coffers - especially those of the industrialized economies, unprecedented financial disparity - with widening gap between the haves and have-nots, wars and conflicts, increasing female

---

[10] Primary name used by the Ottoman Turkey for modern day Istanbul.

infanticide disguised as gender-selection, materialism perverting morality, and an overall lack of trust in the political, financial and religious leaderships; these are some of the factors that demand a review of the modern approach to the social, political, economic and spiritual direction which is wayward and inadequate − unable to maintain ethically correct and socially just course in building the societies.

This book identifies the path that led to the fashioning of the original *Islamic Golden Age*, it also highlights the factors that caused its subsequent decline, and outlines a well considered approach for retracing of the path for shaping of the Golden Age, anew. The approach outlined in this book, if adapted earnestly, will surely reignite mankind's quest for another golden age.

> *Be not, then, faint of heart, and grieve not: for you are bound to rise high if you are [truly] believers. (Qur'an 3:139)*

Chapter Two

Path to Success

❖ *"READ IN THE name of thy Sustainer, who has ● created man out of a germ-cell.● Read - for thy Sustainer is the Most Bountiful One ● who has taught [man] the use of the pen ● taught man what he did not know! ●"* [11]

With the above verses which reminds man of his humble biological origin as well as an affirmation of the gift of consciousness and intellect bestowed on him by the Creator - began, the revelation of the Qur'an to the

------

[11] [Qur'an 96:1 thru 96:5]

Blessed Prophet Muhammad. The process of revelation continued during the next twenty-three years of his prophetic mission and ended shortly before the Blessed Prophet's death, with the following verse:

> ❖ "*AND BE CONSCIOUS of the Day on which you shall be brought back unto God, whereupon every human being shall be repaid in full for what he has earned, and none shall be wronged;*"[12]

"Between these first and last verses in the chronological order of their revelation[13] unfolds a book which, more than any other single phenomenon known to us, has fundamentally affected the religious, social and political history of the world. No other sacred scripture has ever had a similarly immediate impact upon the lives of the people who first heard its message and, through them and the generations that followed them, on the entire course of civilization.

---

[12] [Qur'an 2:281]

[13] The Qur'an, in its final compilation, is arranged in accordance with the inner requirements of its message as a whole, and not in the Chronological order in which the individual passages (Ayats/Surahs) were revealed.

It shook Arabia, and made a nation out of its perennially warring tribes; within a few decades, it spread its world-view far beyond the confines of Arabia and produced the first ideological society known to man; through its insistence on consciousness and knowledge, it engendered among its followers a spirit of intellectual curiosity and independent inquiry, ultimately resulting in that splendid era of learning and scientific research which distinguished the world of Islam at the height of its cultural vigor; and the culture thus fostered by the Qur'an penetrated in countless ways and by-ways into the mind of medieval Europe and gave rise to that revival of Western culture which we call the Renaissance, and thus became in the course of time largely responsible for the birth of what is described as the "age of science": the age in which we are now living."[14]

Through the years when the Qur'an was being revealed, history witnessed an unrivalled transformation of a people - the early Muslims

---

[14] This and the preceding two paragraphs with some alterations are borrowed from the Foreword in the Message of The Qur'an by Muhammad Asad.

who were first to accept the Divine as source of the revelations and who followed its' guidance earnestly, many among them unlearned and inurbane, they were weak and impoverished. Within a few years, the same people had come to be respected as thoughtful and poised, firm and independent. The people who were once persecuted and hunted, now they had become honored and acclaimed.

The course of this transformation was neither easy nor painless. In the beginning these early Muslims experienced intense abuse and persecution. The Meccans boycotted, attacked, imprisoned, and beat anyone who followed the Blessed Prophet. Several groups of the believers had to endure days without food or drink bringing some to their death. As the Muslim ranks grew their persecution also became intensified, some of them were tortured and later killed. Unable to bear these hardships, a group of some two dozen Muslims, migrated to Axum[15] where a benign Christian ruler, king Negus gave them shelter. This was followed,

---

[15] Arabic name **Abyssinia** - (also referred as Aksum)

only two years later, by a second group of about a hundred more, who also had to flee to Axum.

Only thirteen years after the initial revelation was received by the Blessed Prophet, all of the believers including those who had remained in Mecca, were forced to abandon their homes and migrate to Yathrib[16]. Over the next few years, while in Medina, the community remained under repeat attacks from the Meccans and their Bedouin allies. However, the believers' strength in numbers grew steadily, as ever more people from far and wide of the Arabian peninsula, started to accept the revealed message of the Qur'an.

At the time of final exodus from Mecca, it was a weak and defenseless community of about three hundred Muslims. Only eight years later, a ten thousand strong contingent of believers came to perform the pilgrimage in Mecca. Awed by the rapidly expansive impact of the Qur'anic teachings; the chiefs of Mecca

---

[16] Pre Islamic name of Medina; also refereed as *al-Madīnah al-Munawwarah*, "the radiant city" or *madinat al-nabi* "the city of the prophet" - a city in the Hejaz region of what is now known as western Saudi Arabia.

voluntarily handed over control of the city and their own fate to a now empowered and transformed people, who the same chiefs had forced to flee, not too long ago.

The verdict of history is an evident proof that the difference between early Muslims and their persecutors was that while the former accepted guidance of the Qur'an as divinely inspired, the latter rejected it and discarded it as nothing but utterance of a man possessed. The rejecters regarded the revealed message as a work of poetry; they preferred the ways of their forefathers: remaining ignorant, tribal, factious - given to worshipping idol gods, they committed female infanticide - without any regard for accountability and justice, they remained lawless, dealt in usury, and were driven by greed.

On the other hand those who followed the Qur'anic guidance; they came to be characterized as an embodiment of enlightenment and morality, they established a social order based on justice, equity and pluralistic inclusivity, they guarded human rights and practiced gender equality, they banned dealings in usury - respected all life as sacred, they believed in oneness of God and a certain accountability of the life to come.

In short, while the believers recognized the Qur'an as a divine revelation and followed it's guidance; the unbelievers rejected its holy origin and remained defiantly adverse to evaluating it through reason - remaining fixated to the boorish ways of their forefathers. As a result, while the believers were transformed into enlightened people - empowered with Qur'anic wisdom and knowledge, the unbelievers' defiant arrogance resulted in their downfall and the surrender a fait accompli.

The foregoing distinction of outcomes, between the two groups, the believers and the unbelievers, highlights evident impact of the Qur'an, as it proved inarguably to be the sole factor that empowered and transformed generations of Muslims, for centuries, during the epoch known as the *Islamic Golden Age*.

"In the pre-Islamic era, each year tribes from all around the Arabian Peninsula would converge on Mecca, as part of the pilgrimage (Hajj). The exact faith of the tribes was not important at that time, and Christian Arabs were as likely to have made the pilgrimage as the pagans."[17] "Muhammad was known to regularly perform the Umrah,[18] even before he began receiving revelation."[19] Soon after the start of his prophetic mission, at the age of forty, Muhammad (PBUH) was directed, through a Divine Command, to publicly declare the revealed message. Complying, with the Holy Decree, the Blessed Prophet would convey the revealed message to all that he could approach: the locals as well as the pilgrims visiting Mecca.

Within a few years, from the initial revelation of the divine message, people in the peninsula, including inhabitants of Yathrib,[20] (a

---

[17] Karen Armstrong, *Jerusalem: One City, Three Faiths*, p. 221.

[18] A 'minor pilgrimage' to Kaaba in Mecca (like Hajj) which can be performed at any time, and more than once in a year.

[19] Karen Armstrong (2000,2002). *Islam: A Short History*. pp. 10–12

[20] Pre Islamic name of Medina; also referred to as *al-Madīnah al-Munawwarah*, "the radiant city" or *madinat al-nabi* "the city of the prophet", an oasis city in the Hejaz region of Arabia. It's first mention dates to the 6th century

nearby oasis town which later on came to be known as Medina - one of the two holiest cities of Islam), came to know about hitherto revealed guidance of the Qur'an. They learnt about fundamentals of the revealed guidance which emphasizes on upholding of justice, sanctity of human life, dealing with equity and fairness in all social settings, regards charity a core element of the righteous behavior and propagates equality among all human beings - irrespective of their lineage, financial-status, gender and faith.

Prior to the Blessed Prophet's emigration from Mecca, population of Yathrib was a mixture of many different tribes - mainly Pagans and Jewish,[21] who had been fighting for over a century, resulting in an unrelenting civil strife rendering the age-old rules of settling the disputes dysfunctional. In short the city was in dire need for a neutral and trustworthy arbitrator. As they became familiar with the

---

BC. It appears in Assyrian texts (namely, the Nabonidus Chronicle) as Iatribu. In the time of Ptolemy the oasis was known as Lathrippa.

[21] Jews arrived in the 2nd century AD expecting the rise of a prophet there, as foretold in their holy scriptures.

essence of the revealed message, and after three years of mutual consultation among themselves, the inhabitants of Yathrib formally invited the Blessed Prophet and his followers to emigrate to their city. By now, life for the Muslims in Mecca had been made absolutely unbearable, and thus the Blessed Prophet and his fellow Muslims decided to emigrate to Yathrib. It is after this emigration,[22] that Yathrib took on a new identity as Medina.[23]

Soon after his arrival in the city, the Blessed Prophet drafted the *Constitution of Medina,*[24] also known as the *Medina Charter*, a document rooted in teachings of the Qur'an. The charter constituted a formal agreement between the Blessed Prophet Muhammad and all of the tribes and families of what was formerly known as Yathrib, including Muslims, Jews, Christians and pagans. This constitution formed the basis of the first Islamic state. The document was drawn up with the explicit concern of bringing to

---

[22] This journey is known as Hijra or Hijrat.
[23] Originally Yathrib, also known as al-Madina al-Munawara "the radiant city" or Madinat al-Nabi "the city of the prophet"
[24] (Arabic title: Ṣaḥīfat al-Madīnah),

an end the bitter tribal hostility between different clans. To this effect it instituted a number of rights and responsibilities for the Muslim, Jewish, Christian and pagan residents of Medina bringing them all within the fold of a single community: the Ummah.

The *Constitution of Medina* established: the security of the community, religious freedoms, the status of city as a sacred place,[25] the security of women, stable tribal relations within the city, a tax system for supporting the community in time of conflict, parameters for political alliances with outsiders, a system for granting protection of individuals, a judicial system for resolving disputes, and regulations for paying of blood money.

And thus, this *Constitution* – rooted in the values transcribed in the Qur'an, transformed a strife-ridden factious tribal society into an equitable, fair, upright and inclusive model community. All this in less than a decade.

---

[25] Haram: barring all violence and weapons.

The effect of transformation and empowerment, exhibited by the early Muslims of Medina, remained evident through several generations for the initial eight centuries of the Islamic history. The purposes of this book, as stated earlier, is to bring to focus the path that led to the fashioning of the original *Islamic Golden Age.* A few salient examples of the transformational events and milestones, from the early period, are highlighted below to re-emphasize the empowerment process.

First such example is that of the people of Mecca. Prior to accepting Islam they, like other town people, were in a state of Jahiliyya.[26] That is they were generally ignorant, inurbane, uncultured and uncaring. From among these people, a few came to accept divine origin of the Qur'an – and gradually they became believers in the supremacy of its guidance: amongst them were young and old, men and women, rich and poor, free men and slaves. Their acceptance of the Qur'anic guidance was conscious acceptance; based on its appeal to reason, they

---

[26] Jahiliyya is a concept of pre-Islamic "ignorance of divine guidance" or "the state of ignorance of the guidance from God"

submitted after considered deliberation and soul searching. It is due to their conscious submission that the believers remained unwavering in their commitment to the revealed guidance in spite of suffering intimidation and torture. Interestingly, the same very people, the early believers, came to be regarded by their foes and by the history as steadfast, thoughtful, discerning, poised and compassionate.

Emphasis of the Qur'anic guidance on respect for all life as sacred and an incessant stress on upholding of justice - equity - equality and fairness. An unambiguous decree for submission to none except the One God, and proclamation of an unavoidable personal accountability, in a certain life to come with a promise of justice for all. It is such guidance that when accepted consciously, through personal reflection and understanding, manifests itself through transformation of the mindsets and empowerment of individuals. Such transformation and empowerment became an evident trait of many a generations of the Muslims through the initial several centuries of the Islamic Golden Age.

Second example: from the period that must be noted is that of Yathrib, a hamlet which prior to Islam was inhabited by over a dozen diverse tribes, among them Jewish, Pagan and others. After due consideration the tribes invited the Blessed Prophet along with other Muslims of Mecca to emigrate to Yathrib. They saw in the Blessed Prophet an impartial arbitrator, who would judge between them in light of the standard set forth in the Qur'an, as they understood that the revealed criterion made it obligatory for the believers to always uphold equity, justice and fairness. They foresaw a sure salvation for their strife ridden community in the revealed guidance. Their assessment was proven right as within a few years, Yathrib was transformed, from a tribal fractious rivalry into a model society of Medina; symbolizing justice, equity, pluralism and harmony. Over the years, this model became the inspiration cultivating centuries long La Convivencia: a pluralistic interplay between Jews, Christians and Muslims in the famous *Al Andalucia*[27].

---

[27] Refers to Muslim ruled Iberian Peninsula - between 711 and 1492. Though Al Andalus' boundaries kept changing, overall it comprised of the parts of what is today Spain, Portugal, Gibraltar and France.

Third example: the momentous scholastic and intellectual contributions, made during the Islamic Golden age and noted in the chapter titled **Prelude**, are evident proof of the message of the Qur'an which inspired individuals and transformed the mindsets.

For the generations of Muslims who laid foundations for the free flow of ideas and advancement of knowledge; their inspiration was rooted in the Qur'an, as even though all of the intellectuals belonging to the *Islamic Golden Age* originated from diverse geo-linguistic backgrounds, yet virtually all of their individual scholastic and scientific works were chronicled in Arabic - the language they mastered for study of the Qur'an.

Anyone embarking on self study of the Qur'an soon discovers that the divine book encourages critical evaluation, judicious reasoning and contemplation about all matters including the revealed message itself – it is this pattern of study, that in addition to spiritual awakening, often reveals secrets about creation of the universe, laws of nature, development of life, rise and fall of civilizations, and the coming of final cataclysmic event and many other yet-unknown realities. It is obvious that through such contemplative reflection intellectual abilities thrive; a fact made evident by a vast enhancement of knowledge during the *Golden Age* and considerable contributions made by thousands of intellectuals of the Era towards refinement of the human thought.

The preceding three examples, point to the Qur'anic guidance as the sole factor that transformed minds, taking men from ignorance to enlightenment, from disbelief to certainty, from rivalry to harmony and from wayward to virtuous behavior. The divine book guides men to think, reason and deliberate; it promotes nurturing of culture, diversity, steadfastness and courage. In short the revealed message of the Qur'an when approached with an open mind, and heeded to with certain belief, becomes a sure **Path to Success**.

> *"That man can have nothing but what he strives for;"* (Qur'an 53:39 - Abdullah Y. Ali)

Chapter Three

About the Path

❖ *"This [revelation, then,] is a means of insight for mankind, and a guidance and grace unto people who are endowed with inner certainty."*[28]

Previous chapter concluded with examples - highlighting the fact that the Qur'anic guidance is a proven *Path to Success*. Thus, making it incumbent upon all those who claim to believe in the divine origin of the Qur'an, that they study the revealed message consciously and follow its innate guidance earnestly. However,

---

[28] [Qur'an 45:20]

anyone who embarks on study of the divine writ must remain conscious of the fundamental rule elucidated in the following verse:

❖ *"He it is who has bestowed upon thee from on high this divine writ, containing messages that are clear in and by themselves - and these are the essence of the divine writ - as well as others that are allegorical. Now those whose hearts are given to swerving from the truth go after that part of the divine writ which has been expressed in allegory, seeking out [what is bound to create] confusion, and seeking [to arrive at] its final meaning [in an arbitrary manner]; but none save God knows its final meaning. Hence, those who are deeply rooted in knowledge say: "We believe in it; the whole [of the divine writ] is from our Sustainer - albeit none takes this to heart save those who are endowed with insight."* [29]

In order to facilitate man's understanding of the revelation, the Qur'an assigns itself various

---

[29] [Qur'an 3:7]

names (or titles), which signify nature and scope of the revealed message. The following - Table (3:1) - lists these names.

Names of the Qur'an:

#	Transliterated Name	Translation	Qur'anic Reference
1	Al-Kitab	Divine Writ	43:2/44:2
2	Qur'an	Qur'an	56:77
3	Kalam	Word	9:6
4	Nur	Light	4:174
5	Huda	Guidance	10:57/31:32
6	Rahma	Mercy	10:57/10:58
7	Haqq	True	3:62
8	Shifa'	Healing	10:57
9	Maw'iza	Exhortation	10:57
10	Dhikr	Reminder	21:50
11	Karim	Noble	56:77
12	'Ali	Sublime	43:41
13	Hikma	Wisdom	54:5
14	Hakeem	Wise	10:1
15	al-Hadi	Guide	17:9
16	Mubarak	Blessed	38:30
17	Habl	Rope (of Allah)	3:103
18	'Ajab	Marvelous	72:1

Table 3:1 (Part 1 of 2)

Names of the Qur'an: (Contd.)

#	Transliterated Name	Translation	Qur'anic Reference
19	'Ilm	Knowledge	13:37
20	Qayyim	Straight	18:2
21	Qawl	Word	28:51
22	'Arabi	Arabic	39:28
23	Basa'ir	Clear Indications	45:20
24	Bayan	Declaration	3:138
25	Naba' Azim	The Awful Tidings	78:2
26	Tanzil	Revelation	26:192
27	Ruh	Spirit	42:52
28	Wahy	Inspiration	21:45
29	al-Mathani	The Oft-Repeated	15:87
30	Furqan	The Criterion	25:1
31	Fasl	Conclusive, Decisive	86:13
32	Muhaiman	Watcher (i.e. over the past Scriptures)	5:48
33	Ahsan al-Hadeeth	The Fairest of Statements	39:23
34	as-Sirat al-Mustaqim	The Straight Path	6:153

Table 3:1 (Part 2 of 2)

The message of the Qur'an transcends time and space. It unveils for benefit of man, secrets about creation of the universe, and of man's own creation and development through stages, his nature and potentialities. In order to truly benefit from this fount of guidance, one needs to personally read from its original Arabic text, understand, and reflect on, the divine message. It is only after such deliberative process that a person can truly begin to comprehend the Qur'anic wisdom, and thus, follow its guidance consciously and with conviction.

It must be remembered that a few verses of the Qur'an, interspersed in the pages of this book, are only a minuscule sampling of immensity of the knowledge, guidance and wisdom inherent in the revealed message. It is hoped that this sampling may serve as a cursory introduction of the divine writ to those who may be unfamiliar with the revealed message. As for the people, who believe that the Qur'an is merely a religious writ, or such as those who assume that it is a difficult to understand discourse; this sampling may offer a fresh perspective to reassess their own notion about the divine writ.

For the believers, the Qur'an is a unique writ, divine in origin, incorruptible, everlasting and complete. It outlines a sure path for achieving optimum good of this life and the next. It invites man to ponder over the revealed guidance with an open mind, and assures him that when followed earnestly, it will earn him finest rewards in this life as well as in the next. In several passages such as the following, the divine writ describes itself as an unrivaled and unfailing guidance:

❖ *"God bestows from on high the <u>best of all</u> <u>teachings</u> in the shape of a divine writ fully consistent within itself, repeating each statement [of the truth] in manifold forms ......"*[30]

The Qur'an refers to itself as (*Fasl*)[31] "decisive, conclusive" guidance (see Table 3.1), which signifies that the revealed message is a self-sufficient, comprehensive guide, and

---

[30] [Qur'an 39:23]
[31] Table 3:1 - #31 - Page 35

nothing of fundamental importance has been neglected from it. It requires no other discourse, writ, or statements to supplement it. Opposite of the "decisive/conclusive" would be a message that has to rely on supplementary information in order to become decisive or conclusive – an assertion, contrary to the divine writ which repeatedly claims, that it is *"kitabin mubeen"* – meaning that it is *"a clear and self-explanatory writ"*. This divine claim ordains that the reader should seek explanation of the revealed message from within the Qur'an and not look for clarification from elsewhere - for example the following two verses state:

❖ *"Consider this divine writ, clear in itself and clearly showing the truth:"[32]*

❖ *".... A divine writ, with messages that have been made clear in and by themselves, and have been distinctly spelled out as well..."[33]*

"The Qur'an must not be viewed as a compilation of individual injunctions and

---

[32] [Qur'an 43:2]
[33] [Qur'an 11:1]

exhortations but as one integral whole: that is, as an exposition of an ethical doctrine in which every verse and sentence has an intimate bearing on other verses and sentences, all of them clarifying and amplifying one another. Consequently, its real meaning can be grasped only if we correlate every one of the statements with what has been stated elsewhere in its pages, and try to explain its ideas by means of frequent cross references, always subordinating the particular to the general and the incidental to the intrinsic. Whenever this rule is faithfully followed, we realize that the Qur'an is – in the words of Muhammad Abduh[34] – "its own best commentary""[35].

The Qur'an describes itself as (*as-Sirat al-Mustaqim*)[36] "straight path"; a path leading to both temporal as well as everlasting success. As a straight path it promises rewarding outcomes; in the present life and also in the hereafter, iterated in several verses the assurance is directed at all those who earnestly adapt the

---

[34] Also spelled as Moḥammed 'Abduh (1849 – 1905 – Egypt), was an Islamic jurist, scholar and reformer.
[35] The Message of the Qur'an - M. Asad: Foreword page 15 last para
[36] Table 3:1 - #34 - Page 35

proposed path as a modus operandi in their daily life - the revealed message states:

❖ *"As for anyone - be it man or woman - who does righteous deeds, and is a believer withal - him shall We most certainly cause to live a good life, and most certainly shall We grant unto such as these their reward in accordance with the best that they ever did."*[37]

The divine writ also labels itself as (*Furqan*)[38] – "the criterion or the standard" for deciding between right and wrong, true and false, and good and evil. It must be noted that various injunctions that render the divine writ as "the Criterion", and those that distinguish it as the "Straight Path", are interspersed, piecemeal - in varying context, throughout the verses of the Qur'an; which necessitates, that for a fuller comprehension, the revealed message be studied in its entirety. As opinions formed, based on a partial reading, or conclusions drawn

---

[37] [Qur'an 16:97]
[38] Table 3:1 - #30 - Page 35

through selective acceptance of the guidance, may not be valid at all.

The need to consider all aspects of an issue, before reaching a final conclusion, can be illustrated through the example of various revelations explicating characteristics and effect of the "intoxicants". In the Qur'an, there are five different verses that highlight different aspects, as to the nature and the impact, of the intoxicants. The verses are:

❖ *'And [We grant you nourishment] from the fruit of date-palms and vines: from it you derive intoxicants as well as wholesome sustenance - in this, behold, there is a message indeed for people who use their reason !'* [39]

❖ *'They will ask thee about intoxicants and games of chance. Say: "In both there is great evil as well as some benefit for man; but the evil which they cause is greater than the benefit which they bring."'* [40]

---

[39] [Qur'an 16:67]
[40] [Qur'an 2:219]

❖ *'O you who have attained to faith! Do not attempt to pray while you are in a state of drunkenness, [but wait] until you know what you are saying'* [41]

❖ *'By means of intoxicants and games of chance Satan seeks only to sow enmity and hatred among you, and to turn you away from the remembrance of God and from prayer. Will you not, then, desist?'* [42]

❖ *'O you who have attained to faith! Intoxicants, and games of chance, and idolatrous practices, and the divining of the future are but a loathsome evil of Satan's doing:' shun it, then, so that you might attain to a happy state!'* [43]

In order to ascertain Qur'anic guidance as to the impact of intoxication; if only the first three verses from the preceding five are taken into consideration; the conclusion drawn thus, may be significantly different, from that which emerges after weighing in the fourth, and even

---

[41][Qur'an 4:43]
[42] [Qur'an 5:91]
[43] [Qur'an 5:90]

more so, after considering the fifth verse. Likewise, there are many other subjects such as conditions relating to war, acts and types of charity, retribution for murder, punishment for theft, conduct between spouses, laws of inheritance, and so forth; all of which demand that prior to deducing a considered conclusion on any subject matter - the divine writ must be researched, in whole.

The divine writ explains that even though the Qur'anic guidance has been made clear through multiple examples, yet, many among mankind remain unwilling to accept any idea which runs counter to their own mundane tendencies. This fact is iterated in several passages such as the following:

❖ *"For, indeed, many facets have We given in this Qur'an to every kind of lesson [designed] for [the benefit of] mankind! However, most men are unwilling to accept anything but blasphemy"* [44]

and also, the following:

---

[44] [Qur'an 17:89]

❖ *"THUS, INDEED, have We given in this Qur'an many facets to every kind of lesson [designed] for [the benefit of] mankind. However, man is, above all else, always given to contention."* [45]

An example of such a multi-faceted Qur'anic lesson is the phrase: *"God does not burden any human being with more than he is well able to bear"*. This fact is presented in varied contexts, in different verses as shown below:

❖ *"God does not burden any human being with more than he is well able to bear: in his favour shall be whatever good he does, and against him whatever evil he does. "*[46]

❖ *"...No human being shall be burdened with more than he is well able to bear: neither shall a mother be made to suffer because of her child, nor, because of his child, he who has begotten it. ..."*[47]

❖ *"...But those who attain to faith and do righteous deeds - [and] We do not burden*

---

[45] [Qur'an 18:54]
[46] [Qur'an 2:286]
[47] [Qur'an 2:233]

any human being with more than he is
well able to bear - they are destined for
paradise, therein to abide, after We shall
have   removed   whatever   unworthy
thoughts or feelings may have been
[lingering] in their bosoms. ..."[48]

❖ "and do not touch the substance of an
orphan - save to improve it-before he
comes of age. And [in all your dealings]
give full measure and weight, with equity:
[however,] _We do not burden any human_
being with more than he is well able to
bear; and when you voice an opinion, be
just, even though it be [against] one near
of kin. And [always] observe your bond
with God: this has He enjoined upon you,
so that you might keep it in mind."[49]

❖ "And [withal.] _We do not burden any_
human being with more than he is well
able to bear: for with Us is a record that
speaks the truth [about what men do and
can do]; and none shall be wronged."[50]

---

[48] [Qur'an 7:42 - 43]
[49] [Qur'an 6:152]
[50] [Qur'an 23:62]

❖ *"[In all these respects,] let him who has ample means spend in accordance with his amplitude; and let him whose means of subsistence are scanty spend in accordance with what God has given him: God does not burden any human being with more than He has given him - [and it may well be that] God will grant, after hardship, ease."*[51]

The revealed message, at times, accents multiple aspects of guidance through a single theme. For example, a requirement as to essence of prayer is highlighted through a verse already quoted in reference to the effect of intoxication: *"O you who have attained to faith! Do not attempt to pray while you are in a state of drunkenness, [but wait] until you know what you are saying"*.[52]   Here, in addition to highlighting impairment of the mental faculties as a possible consequence of intoxication, it is also decreed that while praying (performing *"salāt"*[53]) the believer must be fully cognizant of

---

[51] [Qur'an 65:7]
[52] [Qur'an 4:43]

[53] Ṣalāt or *ṣalāh* is the practice of formal worship "prayer" in Islam.

(understand) his own utterances, which sheds light on nature and prerequisites of the prayer.

The divine writ also directs the believers to <u>not</u> follow or pursue anything about which one is not sure, or has no knowledge of. As is the case in the following verse:

❖ *"And never concern thyself with [do not follow, pursue] anything of which thou hast no knowledge: ..."*[54]

Commenting on the above verse Asad[55] observes that the command "'*do not follow [or pursue] anything of which thou hast no knowledge*' would seem to relate to groundless assertions about events or people (and hence to slander or false testimony), to statements based on guesswork unsupported by evidence, or to interfering in social situations which one is unable to evaluate correctly." In any case it is necessary that prior to acceptance or rejection of the Qur'anic guidance the revealed message must be critically analyzed, reasoned and understood on personal basis. The divine writ

---

[54] [Qur'an 17:36]
[55] Muhammad Asad whose rendition of the verse is used here.

stresses that man must use reason (sense, understanding) in all affairs of life. In other words, the use of reason by itself is a frequently emphasized Qur'anic commandment, whereas its negation - that is disregard of reason, in matters of faith as well as all other aspects of life, is described in the following verse:

❖ *"Verily, the vilest of all creatures in the sight of God are those deaf, those dumb ones who do not use their reason."* [56]

The divine writ progressively reveals itself, to those who contemplate over its words, magnifying in clarity and expanding in meanings. Also, as a consequence of continued reflection, those attributes of the Qur'an, that deal with man's cognitive aspects such as faith, knowledge, wisdom, truth, inspiration, etc., manifest themselves in an increasingly vivid manner.

An ongoing study of the revealed message, and conscious awareness of its guidance, starts to manifest through the reader's everyday

---

[56] [Qur'an 8:22]

behavior. As a seeker begins to recognize and appreciate the traits that elevate man to his potential greatness, he starts to heed the divine guidance consciously, which in turn sets off a process of his inner transformation. Following is a brief sampling of the Qur'anic guidance, which, when internalized may initiate such a transformational process:

❖ *"...God loves those who are patient in adversity;"* [57]

❖ *"...Verily, God loves those who turn unto Him in repentance and He loves those who keep themselves pure."* [58]

❖ *"...wherein there are men desirous of growing in purity: for God loves all who purify themselves."* [59]

❖ *"And spend [freely] in God's cause, and let not your own hands throw you into destruction; and persevere in doing good: behold, God loves the doers of good."* [60]

---

[57] [Qur'an 3:146]
[58] [Qur'an 2:222]
[59] [Qur'an 9:108]
[60] [Qur'an 2:195]

❖ *"who spend [in His way] in time of plenty and in time of hardship, and hold in check their anger, and pardon their fellow-men because God loves the doers of good;"* [61]

❖ *"...when thou hast decided upon a course of action, place thy trust in God: for, verily, God loves those who place their trust in Him."* [62]

❖ *"...Verily, God loves those who are conscious of Him."* [63]

Likewise, those aspects of human behavior which do not meet the Divine approval must be consciously shunned. An awareness of such negative traits can help man avoid the same and amend own personal behavior. Thus the revealed guidance cautions:

❖ *"...And do not waste [God's bounties]: verily, He does not love the wasteful!-"* [64]

❖ *"...behold, He does not love those who are given to arrogance, - "* [65]

---

[61] [Qur'an 3:134]
[62] [Qur'an 3:159]
[63] [Qur'an 9:4]
[64] [Qur'an 6:141]

❖ *"...behold, God does not love anyone who, out of self-conceit, acts in a boastful manner."* [66]

❖ *"...God does not love evildoers."*[67]

❖ *"...verily, God does not love the treacherous! -"* [68]

❖ *"...God does not - love the spreaders of corruption."* [69]

❖ *"verily, God does not love aggressors."* [70]

❖ *"O YOU who have attained to faith! Do not deprive yourselves of the good things of life which God has made lawful to you, but do not transgress the bounds of what is right: verily, God does not love those who transgress the bounds of what is right."* [71]

---

[65] [Qur'an 16:23]
[66] [Qur'an 31:18]
[67] [Qur'an 3:57]
[68] [Qur'an 8:58]
[69] [Qur'an 5:64]
[70] [Qur'an 2:190]
[71] [Qur'an 5:87]

❖ *"verily, God does not love those who betray their trust and persist in sinful ways."* [72]

❖ *"...verily, God does not love anyone who betrays his trust and is bereft of gratitude."* [73]

❖ *"...And God does not love corruption."* [74]

A person is able to willfully shape own behavior by remaining conscious of the conduct that brings man nearer to the Creator and also being mindful of characteristics which earn Divine displeasure. The revealed guidance also lists certain innate human tendencies that can distract man from attaining true and lasting happiness and therefore one should remain cognizant of; for example the Qur'an cautions:

❖ *"ALLURING unto man is the enjoyment of worldly desires through women, and children, and heaped-up treasures of gold and silver, and horses of high mark, and cattle, and lands. All this may be enjoyed*

---

[72] [Qur'an 4:107]
[73] [Qur'an 22:38]
[74] [Qur'an 2:205]

in the life of this world - but the most beauteous of all goals is with God."[75]

❖ *"But nay, nay, [O men, consider all that you do and fail to do:] you are not generous towards the orphan, and you do not urge one another to feed the needy, and you devour the inheritance [of others] with devouring greed, and you love wealth with boundless love!"* [76]

❖ *"VERILY, towards his Sustainer man is most ungrateful and to this, behold, he [himself] bears witness indeed: for, verily, to the love of wealth is he most ardently devoted."* [77]

The divine writ also warns of conduct that on the surface may seem acceptable, however, in reality is not virtuous, and thus, must be consciously guarded against. Below are just a few examples from otherwise a long list of such practices:

---

[75] [Qur'an 3:14]
[76] [Qur'an 89:17-20]
[77] [Qur'an 100:6-8]

- ❖ *"God does not like any evil to be mentioned openly, unless it be by him who has been wronged (thereby). And God is indeed all-hearing, all-knowing,-"* [78]

- ❖ *"God deprives usurious gains of all blessing, whereas He blesses charitable deeds with manifold increase. And God does not love anyone who is stubbornly ingrate and persists in sinful ways."* [79]

- ❖ *"But [remember that an attempt at] requiting evil may, too, become an evil: hence, whoever pardons [his foe] and makes peace, his reward rests with God - for, verily, He does not love evildoers."* [80]

To enlighten humankind, the revealed message defines the nature of piety or characteristics that constitute the state of being God-conscious. The divine writ states:

- ❖ *"True piety does not consist in turning your faces towards the east or the west - but truly pious is he who believes in God,*

---

[78] [Qur'an 4:148]
[79] [Qur'an 2:276]
[80] [Qur'an 42:40]

and the Last Day; and the angels, and revelation, and the prophets; and spends his substance - however much he himself may cherish it - upon his near of kin, and the orphans, and the needy, and the wayfarer, and the beggars, and for the freeing of human beings from bondage; and is constant in prayer, and renders the purifying dues; and [truly pious are] they who keep their promises whenever they promise, and are patient in misfortune and hardship and in time of peril: it is they that have proved themselves true, and it is they, <u>they who are conscious of God</u>." [81]

Spending from one's material resources is one of the most frequently repeated commands in the Qur'an. The revealed guidance is emphatic in declaring that to become truly God-conscious one must freely and willingly spend for uplift of others in society, even from that portion which is set asides for ones' own needs. Quoted below are a couple of examples from many verses concerning this subject:

---

[81] [Qur'an 2:177]

❖ *"....They ask thee how much they are to spend [in God's cause]; Say: "Whatever is beyond your needs." ...."* [82]

❖ *"[But as for you, O believers,] never shall you attain to true piety unless you spend on others out of <u>what you cherish yourselves</u>; and whatever you spend - verily, God has full knowledge thereof."* [83]

The revealed message has clearly defined role of the Qur'an in the following verse:

❖ *"THIS DIVINE WRIT - let there be no doubt about it is [meant to be] a guidance for all the God-conscious."* [84] -

And then the divine writ singles out one trait that elevates man bringing him nearest to the desired state - of being God conscious:

❖ *".... <u>BE JUST: this is closest to being God-conscious.</u> - "* [85]

---

[82] [Qur'an 2:219 - by Abdullah Yusuf Ali]
[83] [Qur'an 3:92]
[84] [Qur'an 2:2]
[85] [Qur'an 5:8]

The revealed message directs man to reflect on attributes of the Creator as defined in the Qur'an. God's uniqueness, omnipotence and omniscience are described in several verses in the Divine Book, reflection on these and other Divine attributes helps man understand his own role in relation to the Creator and also to others in the realm of the creation.

A certainty of belief in divine origin of the Qur'an leads one to directly seek guidance from the revealed message and heed to its commands. Once this process of direct relationship with the Qur'an becomes a person's faith, it manifests through the believer's enlightenment – as the Divine Writ states:

❖ *"God is near unto those who have faith, taking them out of deep darkness into the light –."* [86]

The revealed message declares "that all good and beautiful things of life - i.e., those which are not expressly prohibited - are lawful to the believers. It condemns, by implication, all forms

---

[86] [Qur'an 2:257]

of life-denying asceticism, world-renunciation and self-mortification. While, in the worldly life, those good things are shared by believers and unbelievers alike, they will be denied to the latter in the hereafter."[87] In this regard the Qur'an decrees:

❖ *"Who is there to forbid the beauty which God has brought forth for His creatures, and the good things from among the means of sustenance?" Say: "They are [lawful] in the life of this world unto all who have attained to faith - to be theirs alone on Resurrection Day." Thus clearly do We spell out these messages unto people of [innate] knowledge!"* [88]

And to explain what is really prohibited, the Divine Writ puts forward the following general guidelines:

❖ *'Say: "Verily, my Sustainer has forbidden only shameful deeds, be they open or secret, and [every kind of] sinning, and unjustified envy, and the ascribing of*

---

[87] Muhammad Asad in his explanatory note about: 7:32
[88] The Qur'an (7:32)

divinity to aught beside Him - since He has never bestowed any warrant therefor from on high and the attributing unto God of aught of which you have no knowledge.'" [89]

The Qur'an is unique in its proven efficacy in terms of transformation, empowerment and enlightenment of the mind, and preparing the man to take up the role of God's vice-regent on earth.

The Divine Book defines patience in adversity and hopefulness as intrinsic traits of a believer – as these qualities personify faith. Whereas hopelessness, despair and weakness of resolve are indicative of straying from the path or non-belief. In fact, being patient in adversity (remaining steadfast) is propounded in more than fifty verses of the Qur'an in manifold contexts. For example, following three verses state:

❖ *"...God is with those who are patient in adversity"*[90]

---

[89] [Qur'an 7:33]
[90] [Qur'an 2:153]

❖ *"And most certainly shall We try you by means of danger, and hunger, and loss of worldly goods, of lives and of [labour's] fruits. But give glad tidings unto those who are patient in adversity"* [91]

❖ *"O you who have attained to faith! Be patient in adversity, and vie in patience with one another, and be ever ready [to do what is right], and remain conscious of God, so that you might attain to a happy state!"* [92]

Whereas the undesirable state of being devoid of hope is depicted in the following two verses:

❖ *"...And who-other than those who have <u>utterly lost their way</u>-could ever abandon the hope of his Sustainer's grace?"* [93]

❖ *"and do not lose hope of God's life-giving mercy: verily, none but people who <u>deny the truth can ever lose hope</u> of God's life-giving mercy."* [94]

---

[91] [Qur'an 2:155]
[92] [Qur'an 3:200]
[93] [Qur'an 15:5 6]

Besides listing many merits of steadfastness and demerits of hopelessness, the divine writ informs man of an everlasting truth in these words:

❖ *"And, behold, with every hardship comes ease: verily, with every hardship comes ease!"* [95]

Composition of the above phrase suggests that "hardship" is one but it comes with two "eases'" – it is sort of like the saying "when one door closes, two more open."

Of all of His countless favors detailed in the Qur'an, God's Grace and Mercy is described in a distinctive manner. As in the verses referenced below:

❖ *"...God, who has willed upon Himself the law of grace and mercy. ..."* [96]

❖ *"...Your Sustainer has willed upon Himself the law of grace and mercy ..."* [97]

---

[94] [Qur'an 12:87]
[95] [Qur'an 94:5- 6]
[96] [Qur'an 6:12]
[97] [Qur'an 6:54]

The expression "God has willed upon Himself as a law" (*kataba `ala nafsihi*) occurs in the Qur'an only twice as shown above -and in both instances with reference to His grace and mercy (*rahmah*); none of the other divine attributes has been similarly described. This exceptional quality of God's grace and mercy is further stressed:

❖ *"...My grace overspreads everything..."* [98]

The verses quoted in this book show a brief glimpse of the type of innate guidance that is part of the revealed message of the Qur'an. This divine guidance when understood through personal circumspection and adhered to earnestly, affects transformation of the mind – it increases man's self awareness and, with Divine Grace, enlightens him with God consciousness.

As many people may have observed in their daily life, that when a law enforcement officer or a patrol vehicle is present on the road, everyone around becomes consciously observant of the traffic regulations. Similarly,

---

[98] [Qur'an 7:156]

through study of the Qur'an, when man actually begins to realize significance of the exhortation that God is Ever-present, All-seeing, All-hearing and All-knowing, he becomes increasingly more conscious of his own actions - with an aim to act rightly (through following the revealed guidance of the Qur'an). This process of self-policing and continued reflection on the message of the Qur'an, increases self-awareness and gradually elevates man where his thoughts and actions, more and more, start to be driven by his consciousness of God. It is this process of individual inner journey, from being unaware to increasingly higher degree of self-awareness - and a persistent effort to act justly, which is the key to transformation and empowerment. It is for this quest that the revealed message of Qur'an is an essential guide. A realization of the importance of the Qur'an as a guide, makes man become eternally grateful for the Divine Mercy, even though he can never be thankful enough.

Although the revealed guidance is universal in its scope, certain aspects of the divine writ are specifically directed towards the believers - to such as those who:

- believe in divine origin of the Qur'an,
- do not ascribe partners in divine powers of God,
- do not turn their face to others besides God in their prayers,
- do not invoke anyone besides God for help, and with <u>inner certainty believe</u> in their frequently repeated proclamation:

> ❖ *"Thee alone do we worship; and unto Thee alone do we turn for aid."* [99]

For the believers role of the Qur'an is pivotal in their life; it directs their behavior in all aspects - from mundane to extraordinary. It details rights and duties of man to the Creator and the creation, it defines his role on earth and clearly sets out the limits of which one must remain conscious of, it presents a path to success for those who heed divine guidance and warns of doom to those who knowingly mutate, neglect or defy it; it is healing and it is light, it is wisdom and it is mercy sublime; it is the most valuable possession the Muslims have; divine in nature,

---

[99] [Qur'an 1:5]

a blessing unique; there is nothing like it – incorruptible and eternal; it is a comprehensive guide for all humankind and not merely a canon of religious dogmas.

> *"Will they not, then, try to understand this Qur'an?"*
> *(Qur'an 4:82)*

Chapter Four

A God-Willed Mission

❖ *"And Thus Have WE willed you to be a community of the middle way, so that your way of life be an example to all mankind, just as the Apostle is an example to you."* [100]

The above verse is a Divine Decree, directing the believers to establish a model community, for benefit of all humankind; a community that is balanced-middlemost, as was demonstrated by the Blessed Prophet himself in

---

[100] [Qur'an 2:143] Rendition by M. Asad modified per his own explanation of the verse - substituting "bear witness to truth" with his explanation "be an example".

Medina. This decree is a God-willed Mission - assigned to those who consciously submit to God, that is who opt to be Muslims.

Further, it must be noted that the acceptance of the God-willed Mission is not an option but is mandatory. Its obligatory nature becomes evident when the consequence of evading the decree or shirking away from the Divine Will is considered. As it has been spelled out, in no uncertain terms, in the following verse, where the believers – those who have avowed to submit to God's Will - are warned:

❖ *"... and if you turn away [from Him], He will cause other people to take your place, and they will not be the likes of you!"* [101]

Referring back to Fiorina's story in the chapter titled **"Prelude"** of this book, she had concluded her lecture with the words:

"In dark and serious times like this, we must affirm our commitment to

---

[101] [Qur'an 47:38]

building societies and institutions that aspire to this kind of greatness."

Here Fiorina was pointing to the inspiration that guided the leadership, stewarding, in her words, the *greatest civilization* – and which she saw to be a model:

"And perhaps we can learn a lesson from this example: It was leadership based on meritocracy, not inheritance. It was leadership that harnessed the full capabilities of a very diverse population that included Christianity, Islamic, and Jewish traditions.

This kind of enlightened leadership — leadership that nurtured culture, sustainability, diversity and courage — led to 800 years of invention and prosperity."

The inspiration for this leadership was rooted in the values prescribed in the Qur'an and as modeled through the very first Islamic community-state, established in Medina by the Blessed Prophet Muhammad.

The Medina model remains to date, a unique example of a society, characterized by morality, enlightenment, and Divine Law. The essential features of such model are: equity and social justice, respect for religious diversity, balance between extremes, realistic appreciation of man's nature and possibilities, rejection of both extravagance and exaggerated somberness. Characteristics that make the society a perfect example to be imitated by all.

The Qur'an reiterates, time and again, that establishment of equity, justice and morality serve as the foundation stones of a sociable community, and commitment to social welfare, rule of reason and quest for knowledge result in its endurance; all six characteristics are vital, a neglect of any one of these factors initiates a process of decline and decay. The Qur'an further elaborates that these values, more than any ritualistic forms of worship on an individual level, are the essence of being a Muslim - and it is such individuals, embodying these values, that are able to shape the model communities - for benefit of all mankind.

The Qur'an defines in detail the parameters necessary for establishing an equitable and just social order. For example, consider the following verse:

❖ *"O YOU WHO have attained to faith! Be ever steadfast in upholding equity, bearing witness to the truth for the sake of God, even though it be against your own selves or your parents and kinsfolk. Whether the person concerned be rich or poor, God's claim takes precedence over [the claims of] either of them. Do not, then, follow your own desires, lest you swerve from justice: for if you distort [the truth], behold, God is indeed aware of all that you do!"*[102]

The greatest civilization, mentioned in the **Prelude** of this book, was influenced by the guidelines as exemplified by the Medina model.

---

[102] [Qur'an 4:135]

After advancing for about eight centuries, this civilization started to falter and its downward slide that started more than six hundred years ago, continues even today.

Concerned with steady deterioration of the Ummah's condition, several Muslim thinkers, have searched for the cause underlying this waning. As a result, many of them, have concluded that the persistent decline is due to "Ummah's forfeiting of the Qur'an as a fount of guidance, knowledge and wisdom". For example, Sir Muhammad Iqbal (1877–1938) - an eminent Muslim philosophical thinker and poet of modern times, highlighted - through his poetry, prose and lectures - vital role of the Qur'an in shaping a Muslim's life. In one of his epic Urdu poem "*Jawab-e-Shikwah (Reply to the Complaint)*", Iqbal accentuates the difference between generations of Muslims of the Islamic Golden Age on the one hand, and those of the modern times on the other, in these words:

وہ زمانے میں معزز تھے مسلماں ہو کر

اور تم خوار ہوئے تارکِ قرآں ہو کر

- o Woh zamanay mei(n) mu'azzaz thay musalman ho kar ~ Aur tum kawar huway taarik-e-Qur'an ho kar

Translation:

- o *"They (your predecessors of yore) were honored in the world because they were Muslims ~ and you (of the recent generations) live disgraced because you have abandoned the Qur'an."*

In another Persian couplet Iqbal emphasizes on pivotal role of the Qur'an, in these words:

- o "Gar tu mi khawhee musalman zeestan ~ Neest mumkin juz ba Qur'an zeestan"

Translation:

- o *"If you desire to be a Muslim ~ (know that) it is not possible except by the Qur'an."*

Through another Urdu couplet Iqbal urges:

- o "Qur'an main ho ghota-zan, aey mard-e-Msualman ~ Allah karey tujh ko at'a jiddat-e-kirdaar"

Translation:

- o *"Dive into study of the Qur'an o Muslim ~ so that Allah may bless you with rejuvenated character."*

Since, the root cause for Ummah's decline has been clearly identified the remedy seems rather obvious – "Return to the Qur'an for guidance and empowerment"; however, without an effective plan to implement the remedy, the decay continues unabated.

Unwilling to make a commitment towards correcting the already identified cause and returning to the Qur'an, the Ummah remains busy in a perpetual hunt for the reasons of the decline. As a consequence of this ongoing search, illiteracy of the Muslim masses is often named as the main factor responsible for their current miserable condition. There is no denying that education is an extremely important factor for societies to prosper; however, in addition to improving the literacy, education must focus on building character as well. It is the character in fact that empowers individuals enabling them to uphold practical application of equity, fairness, ethics and morality in their own selves and their societies. In absence of these values a just social order cannot exist.

Socrates[103], a classical Greek philosopher and teacher is reported to have said: "*If you teach a boy mathematics and fail to teach him character, all in the world you have done is produced a smart thief*".

For the widespread corruption and white collar crimes among most of the modern societies, including those of the so called industrially-advanced Western world, it is the educated professionals such as corporate leaders, business executives, bankers, money managers, politicians, *et al.*, who are generally held responsible for the social-financial ills -- which underscores the crucial role of good character in the life of communities.

As regards the Ummah's state of illiteracy; it can be safely estimated that presently the number of Muslims with college degrees, can be counted in many millions globally, including hundreds of thousands, with higher professional education, such as scientists, mathematicians, academicians, doctors, engineers, economists,

---

[103] (c. 469 BC – 399 BC) a classical Greek Athenian philosopher, credited as one of the founders of Western philosophy,

etc., and yet, the number of new discoveries and inventions, during the last five centuries, that can be attributed to the Muslims is almost negligible.

Interestingly, at the same time, all of the ills plaguing the Ummah, including that of irrelevance in ongoing furtherance of human knowledge, zilch contribution in new scientific discoveries, rampant corruption, bad governance, nepotism and unfair wealth distribution, can all be attributed to the educated class who, as officers and managers, are at the helm of affairs in all segments of the Muslim societies.

Albert Einstein, the genius scientist of the twentieth century is credited with the saying: *"Most people say that it is the intellect which makes a great scientist. They are wrong: it is character"*. He is also reported to have said: *"Weakness of attitude becomes weakness of character"*.

At the dawn of the twenty first century, a general environment of global social unrest, lack of trust in the political, financial and religious systems and leaderships, wars and conflicts, economic inequality, widening gap between the haves and have-nots - all point to the fact that the modern education systems are inadequate in nurturing individuals with ethically correct and socially responsible values.

In recent times, the self-perception of materially advanced societies as bastions of social justice, economic freedom and fairness is being challenged by their neglected populace that finds the facts otherwise, where "We are the 99%" feel entrapped in a tangle of financial bondage; their only hope seems to rest with those who "Occupy Wall Street"[104] or similar occupiers of something else in other places. Presumably, the 1% of these societies, who control the money and wield the power, thinks

---

[104] Occupy Wall Street - a people-powered movement that began on September 17, 2011 in Liberty Square in Manhattan's Financial District, and quickly spread to over 100 cities in the United States and similar actions in over 1,500 cities globally. Through this movement the people were resisting the corrosive power of major banks and multinational corporations over the democratic process, and the role of Wall Street in creating an economic collapse that caused the greatest recession in generations. The movement was inspired by popular uprisings in Egypt and Tunisia, and aimed to fight back against the richest 1% of people that are writing the rules of an unfair global economy that is foreclosing on future of the remaining 99%.

that protest of the 99% is just a fad and that the demand for freedom from the financial bondage and call for social justice will soon vanish. However, the history affirms that the voice of the majority will continue to find new modes of expressions until socio-economic justice comes to prevail globally, and the protestors have wrested freedom from the clutches of exploitative financial systems that keep resurfacing in new forms every few decades. Assuming manifold manifestations, such as communism, socialism, capitalism, materialism, consumerism, and such - these financial systems are designed for accumulation of wealth and power in the hands of a few who are already wealthy and powerful - generally through manipulation.

In the prevailing quick fix environment, where the political and the financial elites are ideologically committed to maintaining the status quo, their solutions are generally designed to produce instant results for the immediate future. What the world really needs is real solutions that are fair and of long term significance.

Present global economic quagmire presents an opportunity for the Muslim economists and thinkers to help realize vision of a different world, a world where economic and financial systems are designed to meet everyone's needs, systems that are free of usury and excessive profiteering, and that aim to bring about equity and fair play - creating sustainable humane societies benefiting the entire humankind.

The Holy Qur'an instructs that in addition to justice, ethics, morality and fairness, other essential ingredients that a model society must incorporate are practice of charity, mercy, compassion and forgiveness. It further elaborates that an enlightened society endures when it learns to appreciate diversity among creation as a manifestation of the God's plan.

Since, achieving *the God-Willed Mission* - that is to establish a model community of the middle way - is dependent upon individual as well as collective communal transformation; the quest to achieve this mission is in fact the journey on the straight path as shown in the Qur'an.

The example set by the Blessed Prophet Muhammad, was explicit and based <u>exclusively</u> <u>on following of the revealed guidance</u>. The holy book testifies to this fact:

❖ "*SAY [O Prophet]: " I BUT follow what is revealed to me.*""[105]

Considering the prevailing chaotic socio-economic environment globally and an even more precarious state of the Muslim Ummah specifically, a refocus on the **God-Willed Mission** is an urgent need. By adopting the already identified sure **Path to Success** i.e. *Return to the Qur'an* - the Ummah can once again transform itself into a balanced community and become a model for the entire humankind, thus presenting a workable solution to the prevailing global chaos. Remember that the Qur'an states:

❖ "*God has promised those of you who have attained to faith and do righteous deeds that, of a certainty, He will cause them to accede to power on earth, even as He*

---

[105] [Qur'an 6:50]

caused [some of] those who lived before them to accede to it; " [106]

God's "promise" contains an indirect hint to the His-Willed natural law which invariably makes the <u>rise and fall of nations dependent on their moral qualities.</u>

The existing global financial state is indicative of a system burdened with inequity, greed and corruption. In such a climate the plight of the Muslims is further aggravated as they have put aside the holy Qur'an as a moral compass, and with that forsaken reason, curiosity, creativity and independent thinking; instead they have adopted conformity with the distorted religiosity as a normative behavior. This reversion to a Jahiliyya[107] like mindset keeps the Muslims from liberating themselves from ignorance and inequity and it renders the Ummah irrelevant in presenting a workable solution for global financial inequity and growing social injustices.

---

[106] [Qur'an 24:55]
[107] The state of pre-Islamic ignorant mindset

Considering *the **God-Willed Mission*** - to be a *balanced middle-most community* and *an example for the entire humankind*, the Ummah has no choice but to Return to the Qur'an, failing which they will remain, as today, an object of universal disgust, dismay and disdain or worst yet earn the Divine Wrath and be replaced by others who will be unlike them.

"*and, verily, this [revelation] shall indeed become [a source of] eminence for thee and thy people: but in time you all will be called to account [for what you have done with it]*."
(Qur'an 43:44)

Chapter Five

Gone Astray!

- ❖ *"VERILY, THIS IS My way, leading straight: follow it: follow not (other) paths: they will scatter you about from His (great) path: thus doth He command you." 108*

To the Muslims - those who willingly submit to the Will of God and who beseech Him in their daily prayers to: *"Show us the straight path"*[109], the verse quoted above is an emphatic command to follow nothing else but the path outlined in the Qur'an <u>exclusively</u>, and to believe with certainty that : *"this is a straight way"*.[110]

---

[108] [Qur'an 6:153 - by Abdullah Yusuf Ali]
[109] [Qur'an 1:6 - by M. Pickthall]
[110] [Qur'an 3:51]

And to remember that:

❖ *"...Verily, God's guidance is the only guidance..."* [111]

The verse quoted at the beginning of this chapter clearly warns Muslims that following all other paths, besides the one prescribed in the Qur'an, will cause them to go astray. That is precisely where Muslims find themselves today: lost, adrift, hopeless, misled, scattered and confounded - in other words they have ***Gone Astray***!

A categorical and unambiguous decree to follow the Qur'anic path exclusively - with certainty and conviction, and to not seek guidance from elsewhere, has been emphasized, time and again, in numerous passages in the Divine Writ — as is the case in the following two verses, quoted here in original Arabic along with respective English language transliteration:

تِلْكَ آيَاتُ اللَّهِ نَتْلُوهَا عَلَيْكَ بِالْحَقِّ فَبِأَيِّ حَدِيثٍ بَعْدَ اللَّهِ وَآيَاتِهِ يُؤْمِنُونَ [112]

---

[111] [Qur'an 6:71]
[112] [Qur'an 45:6 Arabic Text]

- ▪ *"Tilka ayatu Allahi natlooha AAalayka bialhaqqi fabiayyi **hadeethin** baAAda Allahi waayatihi yuminoona"* [113]

- ❖ *"These (ayaat) messages of God do We convey unto thee, setting forth the truth. In what other (hadeeth) tidings / sayings, if not in God's messages, will they, then, believe? "* [114]

فَبِأَيّ حَدِيثٍ بَعْدَهُ يُؤْمِنُونَ [115]

- ❖ *"Fabiayyi **hadeethin** baAAdahu yuminoona"* [116]

- ❖ *"In what other (hadeeth) tidings/ sayings, then, will they, after this (Qur'an), believe?"* [117]

The *greatest civilization* eulogized in the **Prelude** of this book was portrayed as a vast super-state; an empire that "*stretched from ocean to ocean*" and "*within its dominion lived hundreds of millions of people, of different*

---

[113] [Transliteration of 45:6]
[114] [Qur'an 45:6]
[115] [Qur'an 77:50 Arabic Text]
[116] [Transliteration of 77:50]
[117] [Qur'an 77:50]

creeds and ethnic origins"[118] and that *"One of its languages became the universal language of much of the world, the bridge between the peoples of a hundred lands".*[119] The universal language referenced was Arabic – the language of the Qur'an.

For centuries, during the *Islamic Golden Age*, learning the Arabic language - its grammar, vocabulary, idioms and diverse literature - remained a common distinction among learned Muslims and non-Muslims alike. Works produced by the thinkers and the scientists of the Golden Age, regardless of their ethnic origins - from the far reaches of Asia and Africa to the vast expanses of Europe and Al-Andalucía – all favored Arabic as the select language for their intellectual expression.

It is commonly argued that with the Christian West's colonization of the Asian, African and European Muslim lands, the role of Arabic in the colonies was systematically replaced with the dominant colonial languages.

---

[118] Page 6 Para 4
[119] Page 6 Para 5

As a result the language of the Qur'an became a distant, forgotten language in most of these lands and with it went the study of the revealed message from the original text became scant. However, impact of colonization cannot be held solely responsible for the Ummah's prevailing abyss. There are, in fact, a number of intra-communal factors that continue to fuel the Ummah's downward slide.

The main factor obscuring the Ummah's renaissance is the total lack of appreciation that the Qur'an - *"al-kitabi al-hakeem"* - *"a divine writ, full of wisdom"*[120] - is in fact, an inimitable source of guidance and knowledge that leads to the optimum good of the present life in this world. Instead, it is perceived as a religious book - dictating a list of ritualistic dos and don'ts, that primarily concern life in the hereafter. Today's Muslims seek to imitate the industrialized western societies as perfect models of all-around success. A vivid proof of this perception is the fact that to get ahead in life, Muslim countries' educated classes invariably learn at

---

[120] [Qur'an 10:1]

least one Western language but remains illiterate in Arabic., the language of the *"al-quran al-hakeem"* – *"the Qur'an, full of Wisdom."*[121] Interestingly a significant part of this educated class of Muslims - even where their mother tongue is Arabic - hardly ever turn to the Qur'an to seek knowledge and wisdom.

It is in fact the educated class of Muslims who have let Islam be hijacked by a sundry of vested interests. And, it is the same class that has allowed the unscrupulous clergy to portray *Jahiliyyah*[122]-like ignorance and violent behavior as manifestation of the Islamic moral code and social behavior. Furthermore, it is a failure of this very educated class that the Islamophobic campaigns in the West remain largely unchecked. It seems that the so-called educated Muslims are driven only by the want of material success and worldly fame they are awed by the glamour of industrially advanced societies, disregarding the latter's persistent socio-

---

[121] [Qur'an 36:2]

[122] The term **jahiliyyah** denotes the period of a people's - or civilization's - moral ignorance or unconsciousness ; such as in the pre-Islamic Arabia.

economic fissures which yearn in themselves for fresh ideas to escape cyclic upheavals.

Another factor contributing to the distancing of Muslims from the Qur'an is the mushrooming of clergy or Mullahs.[123] In order to insure their own relevance, Mullahs keep reinforcing the notion that to reach proper understanding of the revealed message one has to rely on interpretations from the clergy. By contriving a multitude of peculiar rules about what is Islamic and what is not, and judging between who is a believer and who is not, they continue to avert the average Muslim from regarding the Qur'an as a clear, self explanatory source of Divine guidance, wisdom and knowledge.

It is worth noting that over time different breeds of the clergy have used varying strategies to distract the average Muslim from directly approaching the Qur'an. It is the Mullah who has projected the Qur'an as an esoteric

---

[123] The term **Mullah** is derived from the Arabic word *mawlā*, meaning "vicar," "master" and "guardian" – it is generally used to refer to a Muslim man, educated in theology and sacred law. The term is seldom used in Arabic-speaking areas, where its nearest equivalent is *shaykh* (implying formal theological training).

(mysterious, obscure) book not easily understood by an average person. It is the Mullah again who claims that the revealed guidance is primarily a religious discourse detailing do's and don'ts of the rituals, and which according to him, are not easily discernible without explanations rendered by the clergy or consideration of guidelines established by super clergies of yore. They also scare young Muslims, by claiming that any phonetic mistake made while reading of the Qur'anic text may earn God's wrath - this seemingly simplistic view does great harm as young Muslims, afraid of inviting Divine anger, hold back from approaching the divine book altogether.

Over the past seven centuries, there has existed an ongoing clique between successive scheming rulers and their contemporary cadre of the corrupt Mullah, this in order to keep the common man away from the Qur'an. do you have any sources to support this in footnote? any examples you can point to? Through ever new fabricated projections about the Qur'an, they prevent the average Muslim from being empowered enough to challenge the rulers and the Mullah who continue to usurp peoples' God given rights, possessions and liberties. The distance thus created, between the Qur'an and the average Muslim, continues to be reinforced; through constantly preaching that the revealed guidance should best be left for interpretation with a select group of super-mullahs or the Shaykh who will deduce lessons and pass on to the average seeker.

And behold, the Qur'an refers to itself as *"kitabin mubeenun"*-*"a clear divine writ"*[124], which starkly contradicts the notion that it is "a discourse difficult to understand"; as projected by the clergy and readily accepted by the habitually apathetic cultural-Muslims.

The term "cultural-Muslims" refers to such people who are born in a Muslim family, often with eastern roots, and are brought up in a so-called Muslim cultural environment. An overwhelming majority of these people have never objectively evaluated their own belief system (way of life), and they have never

---

[124] [Qur'an 5:15, 6:59, 10:61, 11:6, 27:1, 27:75, 34:3]

engaged themselves in a personal study of the Qur'an. In other words, they have not opted to be Muslims, it is just that they carry the tag because of their birth. Their values and practices are only a reflection of what their cultural upbringing has transmitted to them – hence the term Cultural-Muslims.

As for such people who consciously opt to be Muslims, –i.e. Muslims by choice, they regard the guidance prescribed in the divine writ as comprehensive and encompassing a complete way of life. Such people consider that the revealed message clearly defines all of the necessary values and forms that must remain permanent, and it leaves out the things that can be adapted as needed to changing times, without compromising essence of the faith.

To illustrate the comprehensive nature of the revealed guidance, a few verses relating to even some seemingly mundane activities such as greeting and not ridiculing others, etiquettes of visiting each others' homes, respecting peoples' privacy, and rules about ablution, are quoted below.

The act of greeting is addressed in more than twenty verses, of which five are being quoted below. These verses are being produced, in their entirety, to demonstrate how diverse aspects of the guidance are often interweaved in a single passage, along with constant reminders of God's Omnipresence, Omnipotence and exhortation for use of reason. These five verses are examples:

❖ *"But <u>when you are greeted with a greeting [of peace], answer with an even better greeting, or [at least] with the like thereof</u>. Verily, God keeps count indeed of all things."*[125]

❖ *"[Hence,] O you who have attained to faith, when you go forth [to war] in God's cause, <u>use your discernment</u>, and do not - out of a desire for the fleeting gains of this worldly life - say unto <u>anyone who offers you the greeting of peace</u>, "Thou art not a believer" for with God there are gains abundant. <u>You, too, were once in the same condition</u> - but God has been*

---

[125] The Qur'an [4:86]

gracious unto you. Use, therefore, your discernment: verily, God is always aware of what you do."[126]

❖ "[ALL OF YOU, O believers, are brethren: [hence.] no blame attaches to the blind, nor does blame attach to the lame, nor does blame attach to the sick [for accepting charity from the hale], and neither to your selves for eating [whatever is offered to you by others, whether it be food obtained] from your [children's] houses, or your fathers' houses, or your mothers' houses, or your brothers' houses, or your sisters' houses, or your paternal uncles' houses, or your paternal aunts' houses, or your maternal uncles' houses, or your maternal aunts' houses, or [houses] the keys whereof are in your charge! or [the house] of any of your friends; nor will you incur any sin by eating in company or separately. But whenever you enter [any of these] houses, greet one another with a blessed, goodly greeting,*

---

[126] The Qur'an [4:94]

as enjoined by God. In this way God makes clear unto you His messages, so that you might [learn to] use your reason."[127]

❖ *"O YOU who have attained to faith! Do not enter houses other than your own unless you have obtained permission and greeted their inmates. This is [enjoined upon you] for your own good, so that you might bear [your mutual rights] in mind."*[128]

❖ *"For, [true] servants of the Most Gracious are [only] they who walk gently on earth, and who, whenever the foolish address them, reply with [words of] peace;"*[129]

All those, whether men or women, who seek guidance from the Qur'an are reminded that they shall never deride, defame or insult one another

❖ *"O YOU who have attained to faith! No men shall deride [other] men: it may well be that those [whom they deride] are better than themselves; and no women*

---

[127] [Qur'an 24:61]
[128] [Qur'an 24:27]
[129] [Qur'an 25:63]

[shall deride other] women: it may well be that those [whom they deride] are better than themselves. And neither shall you defame one another, nor insult one another by [opprobrious] epithets: evil is all imputation of iniquity after [one has attained to] faith; and they who [become guilty thereof and] do not repent - it is they, they who are evildoers!" [130]

As to the proper manners and requisite permission before entering a place — the guidance is:

❖ *"O YOU who have attained to faith! Do not enter houses other than your own unless you have obtained permission and greeted their inmates. This is [enjoined upon you] for your own good, so that you might bear [your mutual rights] in mind. ~ Hence, [even] if you find no one within [the house], do not enter it until you are given leave; and if you are told, "Turn back," then turn back. This will be most conducive to your purity; and God has full*

---

[130] (Qur'an 49:11]

knowledge of all that you do. ~ [On the other hand,] you will incur no sin if you [freely] enter houses not intended for living in but serving a purpose useful to you: but [always remember that] God knows all that you do openly, and all that you would conceal."[131]

And, the following passage focuses on importance of individual's right to privacy:

❖ *"O YOU who have attained to faith! At three times [of day], let [even] those whom you rightfully possess, as well as those from among you who have not yet attained to puberty, ask leave of you [before intruding upon your privacy]: before the prayer of daybreak, and whenever you lay aside your garments in the middle of the day, and after the prayer of nightfall: the three occasions on which your nakedness is likely to be bared. Beyond these [occasions], neither you nor they will incur any sin if they move [freely] about you, attending to [the*

---

[131] [Qur'an 24:27, 28, 29]

needs of] one another. In this way God makes clear unto you His messages: for God is all-knowing, wise! ~ Yet when the children among you attain to puberty, let them ask leave of you [at all times], even as those [who have reached maturity] before them have been enjoined to ask it..." [132]

And as to rather simple seemingly mundane matters such as ablution, the requisite rules and its form have been addressed in two different verses, one of which is quoted below. Again, from these examples alone, it is clear that the Qur'anic guidance is clear, all embracing and complete. As to the requirements and the process of ablution the verse states:

❖ *"O YOU who have attained to faith! When you are about to pray, wash your face, and your hands and arms up to the elbows, and pass your [wet] hands lightly over your head, and [wash] your feet up to the ankles. And if you are in a state requiring total ablution, purify yourselves.*

---

[132] [Qur'an 24:58, 59]

But if you are ill, or are travelling, or have just satisfied a want of nature, or have cohabited with a woman, and can find no water-then take resort to pure dust, passing therewith lightly over your face and your hands. God does not want to impose any hardship on you, but wants to make you pure, and to bestow upon you the full measure of His blessings, so that you might have cause to be grateful."[133]

The preceding nine verses relating to the matters about greeting, defamation, respect for the privacy of others, rule about entry into a house, and ablution - are just a few examples, that highlight the fact that all necessary subjects have been adequately addressed in the Qur'an, and as to the forms or values that have been omitted from a mention in the revealed guidance, it is to enable people to adapt the same to a specific environment, time or individual situation - while ensuring that essence of the rite is kept in view. As the following verse explains:

---

[133] [Qur'an 5:6]

❖ *"O YOU who have attained to faith! Do not ask about matters which, if they were to be made manifest to you [in terms of law], might cause you hardship;...."* [134]

The preceding passage should be read in conjunction with the following two verses, from the same Chapter: [135]

❖ *"No more is the Apostle bound to do than deliver the message. ..."* [136]

❖ *"...Today have I perfected your religious law for you, and have bestowed upon you the full measure of My blessings, and willed that self-surrender unto Me shall be your religion. ..."* [137]

In one of the above quoted verses role of the Blessed Prophet is defined as that of a deliverer of the revealed message and not as a maker of any rules or fashioner of religious rituals. The preceding three verses, when considered together, imply that no one should try to deduce

---

[134] [Qur'an 5:101]
[135] [Chapter Number 5 – titled: *Al-Ma'idah* (The Table Spread)]
[136] [Qur'an 5:99]
[137] [Qur'an 5:3]

"additional" laws from the injunctions besides those that have already been clearly spelled out through the revealed message. The Qur'an states that deducing new rules, that are not already decreed in the divine writ, might in fact become a source of hardship for people -- that is, might (as has indeed happened in the course of the centuries) impose additional burdens on the believers above and beyond anything that has been stipulated in terms of law in the Qur'an.

For those who believe in Divine origin of the Qur'an and consider it as a complete guidance – and about which it has been decreed that it shall remain unadulterated till the eternity; they must understand that the forms and practices intentionally left out of the Qur'an in fact depict a divine favor providing the believers intended flexibility so that they can adapt such forms and practices according to the circumstances. However, over time, this favor has been supplanted by blindly adopting religious concepts, doctrines, assertions and practices preached by no more than the "authority" of mere mortal religious leaders.

The revealed message directs man to use reason in all aspects of life; that is to critically scrutinize even the Qur'anic guidance prior to its acceptance, let alone following another mortal without critical scrutiny. Disregarding the divine decree about using reason, a majority of the cultural-Muslims instead of personally seeking guidance from the Qur'an, rely on the clergy for providing direction as they consider the latter to be authority about all aspects of Islamic knowledge including the Qur'an. In turn, the clergy often develop a formula approach and commit to memory a few passages from the Qur'an that they ritualistically recite at occasions such as deaths, marriages, religious gatherings and Friday sermons, et-cetera. As a result of this careless outsourcing of the Qur'an to the clergy, continued rotting of the Muslim Ummah remains unabated.

A logical consequence of outsourcing of the Qur'an to the clergy has been an increase in sectarianism among Muslims. Emergence of ever new sectarian offshoots, is generally at the behest of a new cadre of clergy who claim to be the only true followers of the faith as interpreted by a specific super clergy or scholar of yore. Albeit, lost in the zeal of obeying dictates of these self righteous clergy, ignoring their fueling of sectarianism, is the divine decree which warns the believers:

❖ *"VERILY, as for those who have broken the unity of their faith and have become sects - thou hast nothing to do with them. ..."* [138]

This verse connects with the following:

❖ *"Verily, this is My way, leading straight: follow it: follow not (other) paths: they will scatter you about from His (great) path: thus doth He command you."* [139]

Even though rampant sectarianism continues unchecked, yet, the Ummah remains heedlessly unmindful of even the most unambiguous, clear and direct divine commands, such as this:

❖ *"Hold fast to the rope of Allah (the Qur'an) all together, and do not separate."* [140]

---

[138] [Qur'an 6:159]
[139] [Qur'an 6:153]
[140] [Qur'an 3:103) English rendition by Aisha Bewley

By abandoning personal study of the Qur'an, which was revealed as a source of complete guidance for each individual believer, the Muslims have deprived themselves from benefit of *the criterion "al-Furqan"* - thus never reflecting on the difference between right and wrong; by ignoring *the wise "al-Hakim"* they remain distant from *the wisdom "hikma";* by not personally reaching for *the light "Nur"* they remain veiled in darkness; by not seeking enlightenment through *the divine knowledge "al-Alim"* they remain immersed in *Jahiliyya* like ignorance; devoid of new learning, unaware of ethics, ignorant of morality, lacking purpose, directionless - they have bartered the divine guidance "<u>*al-Hadi*</u>" for unquestioned compliance to the whims of fallible sectarian clergy. The divine writ questions:

* ❖ *"Will they not, then, ponder over this Qur'an? - or are there locks upon their hearts?"*[141]

Today, the number of Muslims attending the congregational prayers in mosques is at an all

___

[141] [Qur'an 47:24]

time high. However, as a result of outsourcing of the Qur'an to the clergy, a majority of the prayer going Muslims are unable to understand meaning of the verses recited during these prayers. This lack of understanding manifests in individual as well as collective behavior which reflects ignorance of the revealed guidance and is often contrary to the Divine Commands. For instance incessant brutality, unrelenting injustice, rampant inequity, ever-increasing materialism, and disregard for reason, are common everyday occurrences in the so called Muslim societies – all this in spite of clear Divine Commands against such conduct. The Qur'an states:

❖ *"BEHOLD, God enjoins justice, and the doing of good, and generosity towards [one's] fellow-men; and He forbids all that is shameful and <u>all that runs counter to reason</u>, as well as envy; [and] He exhorts you [repeatedly] so that you might bear [all this] in mind."* [142]

---

[142] [Qur'an 16:90]

The Muslims should examine their respective communities to determine if in their society: the *justice* truly prevails? And assess the level of *"generosity towards [one's] fellow-men"*. They should also reflect on their personal behavior and ascertain - that how well they measure in terms of personal compliance to the above quoted divine decree: *"He forbids all that is shameful and all that runs counter to reason, as well as envy"*. The phrase *"counter to reason"* includes ascribing supernatural powers to mortals such as to the prophets, Imams, Saints et cetera, the Qur'an states that all miracles, attributed to the Prophets in the divine writ, happened expressly with God's Will and Permission. In fact, in order to prevent deification of even the Blessed Prophet Muhammad, and to make it clear that he, like all other prophets before him, was only a mortal human being and a creation of God, whom, God had chosen to convey His message to his mankind. The divine writ commands him to clearly deny any claim to supernatural powers:

❖ *"Say [O Prophet]: "I do not say unto you, 'God's treasures are with me,'; nor [do I say], 'I know the things that are beyond the reach of human perception'; nor do I say unto you, 'Behold, I am an angel': I but follow what is revealed to me. ...'"*[143]

The Qur'an repeatedly emphasizes that the Blessed Prophet is only a human being, this to further highlight the fact that no created being, no matter who - has or could ever have, any share, however small or abstract, in any of the God's Divine Powers. As the following verse states:

❖ *"Say [O Prophet]: "It is not within my power to bring benefit to, or avert harm from, myself, except as God may please. And if I knew that which is beyond the reach of human perception, abundant good fortune-would surely have fallen to my lot, and no evil would ever have touched me. I am nothing but a warner, and a herald of glad tidings unto people who will believe."'*[144]

---

[143] [Qur'an 6:50]
[144] [Qur'an 7:188]

The fact that the Ummah, today - is not mindful of the Qur'anic decrees, is an evident proof of a people "**Gone Astray**". And as most of the Muslims are either unable to understand Arabic or they do not take time to study the divine writ, they rely on occasions such as Friday sermons to learn about what they presume to be Islamic values, and, hence, in their mind, guidance originating from the Qur'an. The efficacy of these sermons, it can be reasoned, is evident through the prevailing condition of the Ummah, which is definitely appalling.

A majority of the cultural-Muslims remain oblivious of the fact that the Qur'anic guidance takes humankind from darkness to light and from ignorance to wisdom. They never realize what man's innate potentialities are, and what may eventually become of him, as the following verse reveals:

❖ *"Verily, <u>We create man in the best conformation; and thereafter We reduce him to the lowest of low</u> excepting only such as attain to faith and do good works: and theirs shall be a reward unending!"*[145]

And, since they have outsourced study of the Qur'an to the clergy, the cultural-Muslims never realize that the religious rituals are not an end in themselves. But if anything the rituals are a nominal mean for preparing individuals to achieve the **God Willed Mission**. For it is the mission that is real purpose of a believer's life, as describing the believers the Qur'an states:

❖ *"YOU ARE indeed the best community that has ever been brought forth for [the good of] mankind: ... "*[146]

Considering the prevailing state of the Ummah, is there any who will believe that today's cultural-Muslims, are indeed *"the best community that has ever been brought forth"*? Or, as a previously quoted verse states *"We create man in the best conformation; and thereafter We reduce him to the lowest of low"*[147] - is it unreasonable to conclude that a majority of today's 1.6 billion Muslims, certainly give the impression of being *lowest of the low?* And continuing with the theme, the next verse states

---

[145] [Qur'an 95:4, 5, 6]
[146] [Qur'an 3:110]
[147] [Qur'an 95:4, 5]

"excepting only such as attain to faith and do good works".[148] If a large part of the Muslims seem to symbolize *lowest of the low* – then it clearly signifies that this overwhelming mass lacks in faith and fails to perform good works. In other words; a majority of the cultural-Muslims are in defiance of the divine decrees as most of them are simply ignorant about the Qur'an and unaware of the revealed guidance.

The Qur'an foretells of this eventuality:

❖ *"AND the Messenger will say: 'O my Sustainer! Behold, my people have come to regard this Qur'an as something discarded!'"* [149]

---

[148] [Qur'an 95:6]
[149] [Qur'an 25:30]

Chapter Six

An Eternal Message

❖ *"Behold, thy Lord said to the angels: "I will create a vicegerent on earth. ..."*[150] ~ *"and when I have formed him fully and breathed into him of My spirit, fall down before him in prostration!"* [151]

So begins the story of man's initial creation and his subsequent evolution. Once this creation had attained a preordained form God breathed into him of the Divine Spirit, named him Adam, and proceeded to nurture his intellect - as the Qur'an relates:

---

[150] [Qur'an 2:30 - by Abdullah Yusuf Ali]
[151] [Qur'an 15:29]

❖ *"And We taught Adam the nature of all things;..."* [152]

It is important to note that this course of man's intellectual nurturing - by way of the divine guidance, is ordained to be an incessant process - which began with Adam and is to continue till the end of time.

The Qur'an proclaims that *"... every age has had its revelation"*[153] – and that *"... there never was any community but a warner has [lived and] passed away in its midst... ."*[154] The divine writ further reveals that *"indeed, within every community has God raised up an apostle [entrusted with the message]: 'Worship God, and shun the powers of evil!'... ."*[155] This core decree *"Worship God, and shun the powers of evil"* encompasses the sum-total of all ethical injunctions and prohibitions, as it forms the foundation of all morality and remains the one unchanging message inherent in every bona fide creed.

---

[152] [Qur'an 2:31 - by Abdullah Yusuf Ali]
[153] [Quran 13:38]
[154] [Qur'an 35:24]
[155] [Qur'an 16:36]

The abovementioned core decree remained a common constant, even though, successive apostles, through the ages, received distinct guidance addressing specific issues and circumstances of their own immediate communities - as the Quran states:

❖ *"... Unto every one of you have We appointed a [different] law and way of life. ..."*156

This specificity of *"[different] laws and ways of life"* for different peoples, was perhaps in consideration of moral and intellectual aptitude of the people addressed in each age, and also reflective of humankind's gradual evolution through times. Emphasizing validity of all earlier revelations, the Qur'an asserts:

❖ *"... among the followers of earlier revelation there are upright people, who recite God's messages throughout the night, and prostrate themselves [before Him].~ They believe in God and the Last Day, and enjoin the doing of what is right*

---

156 [Qur'an 5:48]

*and forbid the doing of what is wrong,
and vie with one another in doing good
works: and these are among the
righteous. ~ And whatever good they do,
they shall never be denied the reward
thereof: for, God has full knowledge of
those who are conscious of Him."*[157]

However, according to the divine writ - over
time, each instance of the earlier revelation
became corrupted, rendering the core decree -
"Worship God, and shun the powers of evil"[158]
mostly obscure.

Invariably, the course of corruption of all
earlier writs was caused by human interference
in the revelations, such as supplementing the
revealed message with manmade additions, as
the following verse states:

❖ *"Woe, then, unto those who write down,
with their own hands, [something which
they claim to be] divine writ, and then say.
"This is from God," in order to acquire a
trifling gain thereby; woe, then, unto them*

---

[157] [Qur'an 3:113-115]
[158] [Qur'an 16:36]

for what their hands have written, and woe unto them for all that they may have gained!" [159]

The "trifling gain" mentioned, in the above verse, may have several aspects such as, but not limited to, gaining influence over people by asserting a position of pre-eminence as the alleged "chosen people". This is one example of corruption about human insertions that happened with the followers of Bible.

The Qur'an cautions against certain innate human tendencies that can lead man to an errant behavior. Of note is a subconscious tendency underlying all forms of idolatry and of the attribution of divine qualities to things or beings other than God: in the hope of bringing the Unperceivable closer to one's limited perception by creating a tangible "image" of the Divine Being or, at least, of something that could be conceived of as His "emanation". To draw attention to this tendency the divine writ relates the story of a Samaritan who led a group of Jews to take on worshiping a golden calf as a tangible

---

[159] [Qur'an 2:79]

image of God. The Samaritan also corrupted the revealed message by discarding parts of Prophet Moses' teachings in the latter's absence. The Qur'an narrates:

❖ *"But then, [so they told Moses, the Samaritan] had produced for them [out of the molten gold] the effigy of a calf, which made a lowing sound; and thereupon they said [to one another], "This is your deity, and the deity of Moses-but he has forgotten [his past]."*[160]

❖ *"Said [Moses]: 'What, then, didst thou have in view, O Samaritan?' ~ He answered: 'I have gained insight into something which they were unable to see: and so I took hold of a handful of the Apostle's teachings and cast it away: for thus has my mind prompted me [to act].'"*[161]

Thus we learn that tempting the followers of a revelation into discarding or "casting away" parts of a revealed message is another mode of

---

[160] [Qur'an 20:88]
[161] [Qur'an 20:95-96]

corrupting the revelation through human interference.

The foregoing few verses are a warning to all people, to be mindful of the priests and the scholars. As by adding manmade rules and rejecting certain revealed decrees these scholars were responsible for corrupting the previously revealed scriptures thus misleading their ignorant and unsuspecting followers.

It is only after thousands of years of guided development of man's moral makeup and intellect that the Qur'an was revealed, declaring:

❖ *"And nothing has prevented Us from sending [this message, like the earlier ones,] with miraculous signs [in its wake], save [Our knowledge] that the people of olden times [only too often] gave the lie to them. ~ And never did We send those signs for any other purpose than to convey a warning."*[162]

Explaining his rendition of the foregoing verse, especially its first sentence, Asad[163]

---

[162] [Qur'an 17:59]

writes: "This highly elliptic sentence has a fundamental bearing on the purport of the Qur'an as a whole. In many places the Qur'an stresses the fact that the Prophet Muhammad, despite his being the last and greatest of God's apostles, was not empowered to perform miracles similar to those with which the earlier prophets are said to have reinforced their verbal messages. His only miracle was and is the Qur'an itself - a message perfect in its lucidity and ethical comprehensiveness, destined for all times and all stages of human development, addressed not merely to the feelings but also to the minds of men, open to everyone, whatever his race or social environment, and bound to remain unchanged forever. Since the earlier prophets invariably appealed to their own community and their own time alone, their teachings were, of necessity, circumscribed by the social and intellectual conditions of that particular community and time; and since the people to whom they addressed themselves had not yet reached the stage of independent thinking, those prophets stood in need of

---

[163] [Muhammad Asad - author of "The Message of the Qur'an"

symbolic portents or miracles in order to make the people concerned realize the inner truth of their mission. The message of the Qur'an, on the other hand, was revealed at a time when mankind had reached a degree of maturity which henceforth enabled it to grasp an ideology as such without the aid of those persuasive portents and miraculous demonstrations which in the past, as the above verse points out, only too often gave rise to new, grave misconceptions."

Recounting the whole process of creation, gradual evolution, measured formation and guided realization - the Quran restates:

> ❖ *"'EXTOL the limitless glory of thy Sustainer's name:[the glory of] the Highest,' ~ 'who creates [everything], and thereupon forms it in accordance with what it is meant to be,' ~ 'and who determines the nature [of all that exists], and thereupon guides it [towards its fulfillment], ...'"* [164]

---

[164] [Qur'an 87:1-2-3]

Guiding mankind's development towards realizing the intended fulfillment: that is to transform man's collective mindset where justice instead of inequity, inclusivity instead of exclusivity, meritocracy instead of ancestry, virtue instead of birthright, benevolence instead of hoarding, forgiveness instead of revenge, diversity instead of uniformity, freedom instead of compulsion, and reason instead of blind-faith become the operative norms - is perhaps an objective for which the Qur'an was revealed to the Blessed Prophet Muhammad with the declaration:

❖ *"And unto thee [O Prophet] have We vouchsafed this divine writ, setting forth the truth, confirming the truth of whatever there still remains of earlier revelations and determining what is true therein. ..."*[165]

The Qur'an is a universal message and the Blessed Prophet Muhammad a universal apostle; this proclamation is made in multifold

---

[165] [Qur'an 5:48]

forms in the divine writ - a few example of which follow:

❖ *"Say [O Muhammad]: 'O mankind! Verily, I am an apostle of God to all of you,'..."* [166]

❖ *"This [Qur'an] is no less than a reminder to all mankind • to everyone of you who wills to walk a straight way."* [167]

❖ *"[O MEN!] We have now bestowed upon you from on high a divine writ containing all that you ought to bear in mind will you not, then, use your reason?"* [168]

Like all the previous revelations, the Qur'an is also titled as *Al-Kitab,*[169] which indicates that it includes, the same revelations as was revealed to all the prophets in times past in their original pristine form. Yet, the Qur'an is unique in the sense that it addresses all humankind irrespective of one's ancestry, ethnicity, race, origin and cultural environment; it appeals exclusively to man's reason and, hence, does not

---

[166] [Qur'an 7:158]
[167] [Qur'an 81:27-28]
[168] [Qur'an 21:10]
[169] Table 3:1 - #1 - Page 35

propose any dogmas that must be accepted on the basis of blind faith alone; and also, its incorruptibility has been assured by the Creator Himself.

The fact that - contrary to all other sacred scriptures known to history - the Qur'an has remained entirely unchanged in its wording ever since its revelation over fourteen centuries ago and will, because it is so widely recorded, forever remain so - in accordance with the divine promise:

❖ *"... it is We who shall truly guard it [from all corruption] ."* [170]

For those who believe in holy origin of the Qur'an and such as who have the ability to use reason; the above divine decree affirming safeguarding of the revealed message from all corruption, is enough of a proof that the Qur'an is final, complete and self sufficient guidance.

It is a fact that besides the Qur'an no other sacred text or revered message can claim original purity or perpetual immunity from

---

[170] [Qur'an 15:9]

alteration and corruption. This includes all other texts even from among the Islamic literature such as books about *Sayings and Traditions of the Blessed Prophet Muhammad*. It is widely recorded that with the sole exception of his *Farewell Pilgrimage Sermon*,[171] the Blessed Prophet warned people against writing any of his utterances unless such be identified, personally by him, as the Qur'anic revelations. As an example we can review the case of this *Farewell Sermon* which was delivered at about the same time as the final few verses of the Qur'an were revealed. It is widely reported that the *Farewell Sermon* was delivered in front of tens of thousands of Muslims. Below are brief excepts from an account of the sermon which was collected by an early historian.[172] According to this account the Blessed Prophet after he had praised and Glorified God - said:

---

[171] *the Farewell Pilgrimage Sermon of the Blessed Prophet Muhammad,* delivered in Mecca on 9th of Dhu al-Hiijah, 10 AH (9 March 632).

[172] Ibn Ishaq, as quoted in Ibn Hisham's Sirahan-Nabawiyah and at-Tabari's Tarikh, with minor differences. The narration is translated by I. K. Poonawala in The History of al-Tabari, vol. IX: The Last Years of the Prophet (1990).

"Oh, people! Lend me an attentive ear, for I know not whether after this year, I shall ever be amongst you again. Therefore listen to what I am saying to you very carefully and take these words to those who could not be present here today. ..."

After this clear advice to the audience the Blessed Prophet continued with highlighting important elements of individual as well as collective Muslim behavior. Notwithstanding with his clear instructions "to carefully listen to and convey his words to those who were not present" there exist at least six different versions of the *Farewell Sermon*. These different versions can be found in various books including well known Hadeeth works of respected scholars such as of Bukhari,[173] Muslim,[174] Ibn-e-Majah,[175] Ahmed bin Hanbal,[176] etc. – each quoting somewhat different version in his collection. Some of the differences between the

---

[173] Muhammad al-Bukhari (810 – 870) author of Sahih al- Bukhari.

[174] Muslim ibn al-Ḥajjāj (815 – 875) author of Sahih Muslim.

[175] Muḥammad Ibn Mājah (824-887) author of Sunan Ibn Majah.

[173] Ahmad ibn Hanbal (780–855) author of Musnad Ahmad ibn Hanbal.

six widely circulated versions are significant and profound. For instance towards the end of this sermon the Blessed Prophet is reported to have advised the assembly to hold fast to what he is leaving behind lest they go astray. One version, has the statement: "*I leave for you the Qur'an, you shall uphold it.*" The other version has the statement: "*I leave with you Qur'an and my Sunnah*[177]". The third version has the statement: "*I leave with you Qur'an and Ahl al-bayt*[178]". And yet another version states: "*I leave behind the Qur'an, my Sunnah and Ahl al-bayt*". Considering the Blessed Prophet's rather emphatic advice to the audience to make note of his words and to convey the same to those who were not present, we find that the words and the essence of his *Final Sermon* changed within three hundred years of the event. This is an evident proof that besides the Qur'an there is no other text, no matter how revered, which can claim unadulterated original purity.

It is by virtue of all of the foregoing factors that the Qur'an represents the final stage of all

---

[177] Sunnah denotes practices of the Blessed Prophet Muhammad.
[178] Family of the Blessed Prophet Muhammad.

divine revelations. And it is for this reason that the Blessed Prophet Muhammad, through whom the Quran was revealed, is described in the divine writ as an evidence of *"... [God's] grace towards all the worlds (i.e. towards entire mankind)."*[179]

It has been illustrated through the pages of this book that the Qur'anic guidance is a sure *path to success.* It has also been highlighted that not only is the divine writ protected against all forms of adulteration but is also safe from any type of shadiness that may obscure its meaning - rendering the Qur'an as an easy to understand writ. As the revealed message states:

❖ *"ALL PRAISE is due to God, who has bestowed. this divine writ from on high upon His servant, and has not allowed any deviousness to obscure its meaning."* [180]

While recounting initial creation and evolution it was noted that nurturing of the man's intellect through the divine guidance began with Adam, and is decreed to remain so

---

[179] [Qur'an 21:107]
[180] [Qur'an 18:1]

till the end of time, as affirmed by Prophet Ibrahim quoting whom the divine writ states:

❖ "[The Sustainer of all the worlds] who has created me is the One who guides me " [181]

A firm belief that the Qur'an is the final revelation and the Blessed Prophet Muhammad the seal of all the prophets means that the Qur'an must be perceived as original, complete, self-sufficient, unambiguous and preserved guidance to remain so till eternity. It is obvious that for a guidance to be eternal it must always stay unchanged, be incorruptible, remain constant and be complete. Those who believe in divinity of the revealed message of the Qur'an also understand that if any additional resource was at all necessary for ongoing moral guidance of humankind, then the Blessed Prophet Muhammad would have ensured recording and preservation of such a resource, like that of the Qur'an, with Divine Guarantees against its adulteration and corruption.

---

[181] [Qur'an 26:78 Asad modified]

Testifying to the timeless and universal character of the Qur'an - God reveals that ever new significance, meaning and purpose of the revealed message will continue to emerge, and the process is to continue, until the end of time:

❖ *"This [divine writ], behold, is no less than a reminder to all the worlds - and you will most certainly grasp its purport after a lapse of time!"* [182]

> "O MANKIND! There has now come unto you an admonition from your Sustainer, and a cure for all [the ill] that may be in men's hearts,...."
>
> *(Qur'an 10:57)*

---

[182] [Qur'an 38:87 - 88]

Chapter Seven

Retracing the Path

❖ *"...Now there has come unto you from God a light, and a clear divine writ, through which God shows unto all that seek His goodly acceptance the paths leading to salvation and, by His grace, brings them out of the depths of darkness into the light and guides them onto a straight way."*[183]

The Qur'an is an incomparable discourse. It provides guidance and enlightenment. It transforms and empowers individuals. For those

---

[183] [Qur'an 5:15-16]

who have faith and heed to the divine guidance the Qur'an presents a sure *path to success* - both in this life and the next. And yet, the Muslims who are ever ready to exert a claim on the Qur'an are, in fact, unable or unwilling to read the book for seeking guidance, knowledge and wisdom.

While continuing to live in a state of self deception, the cultural Muslims believe that their pathetically haphazard existence is in fact according to the divine rules. It is about time that they come to realize that their meaningless survival continues to take them further downwards, and that their individual as well as collective revival is dependent exclusively upon a determined return to the Qur'an.

The revival entails that all those who believe in the Qur'an must commit to a regular conscious study of the revealed message with an objective to seek guidance, knowledge and wisdom. Also, they must heed to personally understood guidance earnestly. This approach is in essence **retracing the path** to success as it leads to transformation and empowerment of all those who consciously adopt the revealed guidance, enabling them to pursue the **God Willed Mission -** as stated in the verse below:

> ❖ *"And Thus Have WE willed you to be a community of the middle way, so that your <u>way of life</u> be an example to all mankind..."* [184]

The term <u>way of life</u> in the above verse, is a collective expression encompassing the social and individual, as well as the spiritual and material, aspects of human existence. According to the Qur'an all these four aspects form one indivisible whole and cannot, therefore, be dealt with independently of one another. The Qur'an deliberately interweaves moral exhortation with practical legislation to pursue the teaching that all facets of man's life – spiritual and physical, individual and social - is one integral whole, and therefore requires simultaneous consideration of all its aspects. Thus it is important to remember that only a wholesome approach,

---

[184] [Qur'an 2:143] Rendition by M. Asad modified per his own explanation of the verse - substituting "bear witness to truth" with his explanation "be an example".

encompassing all aspects of life, is the key for a fulfilling journey on the **Path to Success**.

For those who are new to the Qur'an, listed below are a few suggestions that may facilitate their study of the divine writ:

To begin with one must take a special note of the divine decree:

❖ "...*Verily, God's guidance is the only guidance ...*" [185]

And also, remember that this guidance is a consequence of God's Grace, bestowed on those who are sincere in their quest to be guided, as is evident through the following verse:

❖ *"For, had God so willed, He could surely have made you all mankind one single community; however, He lets go astray him that wills [to go astray], and guides aright him that wills [to be guided];..."* [186]

Therefore, only when man resolves to sincerely adapt a virtuous course, through his

---

[185] [Qur'an 6:71]
[186] [Qur'an 16:93]

actual conduct, the Divine Grace guides him on the path leading to success. Conversely, if one defiantly sets out on pursuing his own temporal lusts, then God lets him go on his chosen way.

Also, it must be noted that whenever man decides to pursue the right course, invariably, the evil forces become active to distract him. Therefore, the divine writ guides the seekers:

❖ *"NOW whenever thou happen to read this Qur'an, seek refuge with God from Satan, the accursed."* [187]

And, it is important that the divine writ be approached with an open mind - weighing each word critically, to seek guidance and wisdom, and discarding all previously held concepts and biases. The seeker must embrace self reflection, adopt self scrutiny, always be ready to learn what is right, and to adjust his or her own course accordingly.

The Qur'an asserts that the revealed message is a clear and easy to understand

---

[187] [Qur'an 16:98]

discourse. In fact the following verse is repeated multiple times in the divine writ:

❖ *"And We have indeed made the Qur'an easy to understand and remember..."* [188]

The Quran refers to itself as *Alkitabi Almubeen* - which can be rendered into English as: *"divine writ, clear in itself and clearly showing the truth"*[189]. This oft-repeated title underscores the self explanatory nature of the divine writ as it suggests that the Qur'an is its own best commentary. This fact is further illustrated by the following verse:

❖ *"... God makes [His] messages clear unto you..."*[190]

A self-explanatory nature of the Qur'an implies that any ambiguity about any word (or theme) of the revealed message can be resolved through reviewing other occurrences of the same word in the divine writ and thus deriving an appropriate meaning (or sense) holistically. In order to find other occurrences of an Arabic

---

[188] [Qur'an 54:17, 22, 32, 40 by Abdullah Yusuf Ali]
[189] [Qur'an 43:2, 44:2 and 12:1, 26:2, 28:2 with slight variation]
[190] [Qur'an 24:18]

word, *concordances of the Qur'an* can be utilized, which are readily available in most major languages. The Qur'an emphasizes:

❖ *"...Unto all who have attained to faith, this [divine writ] is a guidance and a source of health; but as for those who will not believe - in their ears is deafness, and so it remains obscure to them: they are [like people who are] being called from too far away.* [191]

A crucial factor in the study of the Qur'an is a consideration for the language of the revelation, as it has been highlighted through several verses - such as in the following example:

❖ *"behold, We have bestowed it from on high as a discourse in the Arabic tongue, so that you might encompass it with your reason."* [192]

Over the centuries, linguists and scholars have concluded that the Qur'an is an

---

[191] [Qur'an 41:44]
[192] [Qur'an 12:2]

untranslatable discourse as no one translation can capture the nuance and meanings of each verse. Also, considering that the message of the Qur'an transcends time and space – it necessitates a perpetual need for fresh reinterpretation of the revealed message. The fact that every interpretation is time-bound i.e. it is based on, at the time, prevailing human knowledge and personal biases, it remains limited in perspective - unable to transmit an all-encompassing scope and meaning, which invariably results in an ongoing review of the existing renditions and consequent emergence of ever new interpretations. The Qur'an itself prompts for a perpetual quest to study and interpret the revealed message afresh:

❖ *"This [divine writ], behold, is no less than a reminder to all the worlds - and you will most certainly grasp its purport after a lapse of time!"* [193]

Anyone embarking on a serious study of the Qur'an concludes that the knowledge of Arabic is essential. However, if one does not know or

---

[193] [Qur'an 38:87 - 88]

understand Arabic it is important to know a few basic facts about the Arabic language.

Arabic is a very structured language, in which the meaning of a word is based on its roots, which usually consist of three letters. Variations in shades of meaning are obtained, first by vowelling the simple root, and secondly by the addition of prefixes, suffixes and in-fixes. When one has become familiar with structure of the language and learned various derived forms of the verbs, one can use an Arabic dictionary with ease, as all Arabic dictionaries enter words under their roots and only the roots are in alphabetical order. So those who have some grounding in the language can easily find the meaning of an Arabic word from its roots by consulting an Arabic-English dictionary or lexicon. For those who are interested in a deeper understanding of the Qur'an, it would be useful to have a concordance of the Qur'an, which lists all the verses in which a particular word appears, together with its root.

It needs to be re-emphasized that for a deeper understanding of the Qur'an, some basic knowledge of the Arabic language is absolutely essential.

As to approach through the English language renditions, more than fifty different such translations are accessible on the internet. In fact, as of the first publication in 2014 of this book, forty eight such titles can be found on one website alone.[194] Several other websites also host multiple interpretations. Links to some of these works are listed in the useful links page towards the end of this book.

Each translations varies slightly throughout as each translator must insert his or her own words in parenthesis to facilitate capturing the meaning of the verse lost in translation.

The fact that all these translations may be erroneous becomes evident as one studies multiple renditions and discovers that different people have understood the message quite differently. Thus, it becomes necessary that a reader who studies message of the Qur'an through other language interpretations must

---

[194] www.islamawakened.com/quran, http://al-quran.info/

consult as many renditions as possible in order to get a fairer sense of the original message. Even then one must always remain conscious of the fact that whatever one is reading is, in fact, an extremely limited rendition of a timeless and vast message, as every interpretation is filtered through finite understanding of a human being. Also, one must be aware of the fact that such translations and interpretations may not, always, communicate correct meanings and are never able to convey complete import of the revealed message.

To highlight how different renditions may vary, quoted below are three different renditions of verse 17 of chapter 88:

- ❖ *"Do they not look at the Camels, how they are made?- "* (by Abdullah Y. Ali)

- ❖ *"Will they not regard the camels, how they are created?"* (*Marmaduke* Pickthall)

- ❖ *"DO, THEN, they [who deny resurrection] never gaze at the clouds pregnant with water, [and observe] how they are created? "* (by Muhammad Asad)

In the first two renditions above, the original Qur'anic noun *ibil* has been translated as *camels* whereas, in the third instance it has been rendered as *clouds pregnant with water*. Explaining his interpretation Asad notes: "As regards the noun *ibil*, it denotes, as a rule, *camels*: a generic plural which has no singular form. But one must remember that it also signifies *clouds bearing rain-water* (Lisan al-'Arab, Qamus, Taj al-'Arus) - a meaning which is preferable in the present context. He further justifies his interpretation in light of the subject being addressed in the context considering the previous sixteen and the subsequent three verses although two of the three texts quoted use the word "camel" consideration of the text of Asad's translation appears to make the most sense. Asad's rendition of all of these twenty verses (88:1 through 88:20) is being presented below so that the readers can see the veracity of his argument:

❖ *"HAS THERE COME unto thee the tiding of the Overshadowing Event?' Some faces will on that Day be downcast, toiling [under burdens of sin], worn out [by fear],* about to enter a glowing fire, given to drink from a boiling spring. No food for them save the bitterness of dry thorns, which gives no strength and neither stills hunger." (88:1-7)

❖ "[And] some faces will on that Day shine with bliss, well-pleased with [the fruit of] their striving, in a garden sublime, wherein thou wilt hear no empty talk. Countless springs will flow therein, [and] there will be thrones [of happiness] raised high, and goblets placed ready, and cushions ranged, and carpets spread out..."(88:8-16)

❖ "DO, THEN, they [who deny resurrection] never gaze at the clouds pregnant with water, [and observe] how they are created?" (88:17)

❖ "And at the sky, how it is raised aloft? And at the mountains, how firmly they are reared? And at the earth, how it is spread out?" (88:18-20)

To illustrate significant differences in various interpretation, another example (of verse 47 of chapter 51) is given below:

❖ *"With power and skill did We construct the Firmament: <u>for it is We Who create the vastness of space.</u>"* (by Abdullah Y. Ali)

❖ *"We have built the heaven with might, and <u>We it is who make the vast extent (thereof)</u>."* (by Marmaduke Pickthall)

❖ *"And it is We who have built the universe with [Our creative] power; and, verily, <u>it is We who are steadily expanding it</u>."* (by Muhammad Asad)

The Arabic phase *"inna lamoosi- AAoona"* which is part of the verse 51:47 has been interpreted differently in the three renditions quoted above. The noted differences are based on varied perception of the translators, about the creation of the universe and it's related phenomena – such as the vastness of the universe, whether it is fixed in its extent or continually expanding. Explaining his rendition, Asad explains that the phrase *"inna lamoosi-*

AAoona" clearly foreshadows the modern notion of the "expanding universe" - that is, the fact that the cosmos, though finite in extent, is continuously expanding in space.

Considering the two examples presented above, it is obvious that all interpretations may in fact be imperfect as all of these are time bound while God's word is eternal. Invariably, the time-bounded nature of interpretations includes all languages – thus, anyone who seeks the divine guidance in its pristine form, must seek it through Arabic – the original language of the revelation.

It is a well established fact that even the works of poetry, such as that of Rumi, when rendered from an eastern language to English, transfers only a limited scope of the original thought. All renditions are invariably confined in scope by the personal understanding of the subject matter by the translator and also by limitations of the target language. Therefore, for a comprehensive unrestricted understanding of the Qur'an, approach to its innate wisdom, knowledge, and guidance must be sought through the original Arabic text.

The reader must also be aware that penetrating study of the Qur'an, at times, may unveil new meaning of certain aspects of the revealed message. These new meanings may differ, from what other people project or may have understood in the past. However, such new meaning must not be discarded automatically. Instead, it should be scrutinized further for its rationale and appropriateness. The fact is that it is only through probing studies that human knowledge may expand; and at times, formerly unknown secrets about the universe are discovered.

The following is an example of how relying on interpretations limits the scope of the revealed message, and thus may mislead and impair the advancement of human knowledge. Below is the original Arabic text with transliteration of verse 30:3:

"فِي أَدْنَى الأَرْضِ وَهُم مِّن بَعْدِ غَلَبِهِمْ سَيَغْلِبُونَ "

Transliteration: *"Fee **adna alardi** wahum min baAAdi ghalabihim sayaghliboona"*

Asad's Translation: *"in the lands close-by; yet it is they who, notwithstanding this their defeat, shall be victorious"*

For the purpose of this illustration, the English language rendition of the two Arabic words **adna alardi** was compared by examining thirty-six different English translations available on a website.[195] All but one translation rendered essentially similar meanings of these two words. The commonly given meanings are: *"land nearby, land close by, neighboring land, nearby territory, nearer part of land, your neighborhood, nearer land, nighest parts of the land, nearest part of the land, near land, land hard by, the land's/planet Earth's nearest, more adjacent (i.e., more easy to reach; the Levant) (part) of the earth, the nearest front"*. The one differing rendition gave the meaning: "**lowest point on Earth**". This differing interpretation is found in the rendition titled "The Qur'an - A Monotheist Translation". It is important to note that all major Arabic-English lexicons list "lowest or low" as one meaning(s) of the word **adna**.

---

[195] http://al-quran.info (Online Qur'anic Project)

Verses 30:2 and 30:3 describe the outcome of a battle between the Romans and the Persians which, according to history books, took place in the Dead Sea area in 615/616 CE. Based on recent advances since the 1900s in the field of physical geography, man has learned that the Dead Sea shore is the **lowest** point on Earth.

Perhaps, if all different meanings of the these two words *'adna alardi'* had been considered by some Muslim scientist anytime during the past thirteen centuries, prior to the recent developments in the field of physical geography, mankind could have possibly discovered Earth's elevation levels and related sciences sooner.

Many of the scientific discoveries that the modern day Muslims proudly claim as a proof of divine origin of the Qur'an should actually put the Ummah to shame. In spite of the claims that such scientific truth and other wisdoms are vouchsafed in the Qur'an-al Hakim (Book of Wisdom) modern day Muslims count for naught in the field of new discoveries and furtherance of knowledge. It is evident that to discover yet uncovered secrets that may be present in the divine writ, the seeker of knowledge and wisdom must reinterpret every word of the Qur'an in light of the latest human knowledge and most recent scientific data.

When the Muslims decide to approach the Qur'an afresh with an open mind, while seeking guidance, knowledge, and wisdom, considering all possible meanings of every original Arabic word of the text, evaluating its applicability, and heeding to the divine guidance earnestly; it is only then that they may regain the position of leadership they once held, in the fields of knowledge, innovation, discovery, and social sciences.

A focused seeker of guidance, knowledge and wisdom must also keep in mind the following:

- When studying the Qur'an - <u>the context of the verse</u> must be kept in focus and each verse must be viewed in its entirety. By ignoring its context or by considering only part of the verse in isolation, one is able to justify otherwise totally unwarranted meanings. The context, in this case, includes review of all related (immediately before and immediately after) verses for a better and appropriate understanding of the subject matter.

■ The Qur'an lauds people who follow the evidence supplied by their own reason and who reach their conclusions in accordance with the results of critical examination and logical inference. This commendation is to encourage the use of reason and acceptance of that which one's mind finds to be valid, possible, and rejecting all that does not measure up to the test of reason. The people who weigh multiple options and select the one that appeals to the reason are mentioned in the following verse:

❖ *"Who listen [closely] to all that is said, and follow the best of it: [for] it is they whom God has graced with His guidance, and it is they who are [truly] endowed with insight!"*[196]

- Those who engage in study of the divine writ should let the Qur'an reveal itself, gradually, just as it was revealed to the earliest Muslims — that is to the contemporaries of the Blessed Prophet Muhammad. This is only possible when the learner keeps an open mind and does not hold on to pre-conceived notions about the revelations.

- A seeker of truth must also realize that whatever is conceivable is achievable as it may have bearing on understanding certain phenomenon that may otherwise seem impossible or miraculous in nature. However, over time, with advancement of human knowledge, many such things may become evidently clear.

Finally, everyone must take a special note the Qur'anic decree:

- ❖ "... *Become men of God by spreading the knowledge of the divine writ, and by your own deep study [thereof].*"[197]

---

[196] [Qur'an 39:18]
[197] [Qur'an 3:79]

In conclusion, those who affirm that the Qur'an is indeed a divine message, that it details a complete guidance for life, and that it defines a sure path to success - they must:

- Believe in it completely
- Read it regularly
- Understand what it says
- Reflect and ponder on its message
- Act upon its guidance and
- Spread its knowledge

"...They [who understand this message -it is they alone who truly] believe in it;..." *(Qur'an 11:17)*

Chapter Eight

A New Golden Age

❖ *"To a happy state shall indeed attain he who causes the human self to grow in purity, ~ and truly lost is he who buries it [in darkness]."* [198]

Referring back to the summit held under auspices of the *World Islamic Economic Forum,* as mentioned in the chapter titled **Prelude** of this book, a group of Islamic nations had expressed a need to create a *New Golden Age.* This yearning for a renaissance becomes more pronounced when we consider a progressively

---

[198] [Qur'an 91:9-10]

deteriorating social, political and economic world order, where a huge segment of humanity suffers from growing poverty with widening gap between the haves and have-nots, and where injustice and abuse of human rights is filtered through the prism of might is right.

As described in chapter One of this book, in narrating story of the greatest civilization Fiorina had remarked:

"Although we are often unaware of our indebtedness to this other civilization, its gifts are very much a part of our heritage. The technology industry would not exist without the contributions of Arab mathematicians. Sufi poet-philosophers like Rumi challenged our notions of self and truth. Leaders like Suleiman contributed to our notions of tolerance and civic leadership.

And perhaps we can learn a lesson from his example: It was leadership based on meritocracy, not inheritance. It was leadership that harnessed the full capabilities of a very diverse population that included Christianity, Islamic, and Jewish traditions.

This kind of enlightened leadership — leadership that nurtured culture, sustainability, diversity and courage — led to 800 years of invention and prosperity."

Through the pages of this book it has been established that following the Qur'anic guidance is indeed a proven path to success. It is this path that early Muslims had followed. Thus, in order to reshape a New Golden Age there is no alternative but to once again adopt the path defined in the Qur'an, earnestly, which invariably transforms and empowers anyone who is willing to heed the advice. The divine writ states:

❖ *"... and he who follows My guidance will not go astray, and neither will he be unhappy."* [199]

And then it implores:

---

[199] [Qur'an 20:123]

❖ *"Hence, indeed, We made this Qur'an easy to bear in mind: who, then, is willing to take it to heart?"*[200]

The divine writ also forewarns of an inescapable loss or failure unless man comes to personify certain key characteristics that are, in fact, essential ingredients for success. The Qur'an declares:

❖ *"CONSIDER the flight of time! ~ Verily, man is bound to lose himself ~ unless he be of those who attain to faith, and do good works, and enjoin upon one another the keeping to truth, and enjoin upon one another patience in adversity."* [201]

"O our Sustainer! Bestow on us grace from Thyself, and endow us, whatever our [outward] condition, with consciousness of what is right!" (Qur'an 18:10)

---

[200] [Qur'an 54:17]
[201] [Qur'an 103:1-2-3]

ONLINE RESOURCES

Following are a few links to some useful online resource for study of the Qur'an.

www.islamicity.com

www.thequranstudy.org

www.islamawakened.com/quran

http://corpus.quran.com/wordbyword.jsp?

http://www.studyquran.co.uk/PRLonline.htm

www.al-quran.info

www.UMMA2020.com

ABOUT THE AUTHOR

After graduating, in 1967, from the Emerson College, Multan, Pakistan, with a BS degree in Biology, the author received computer programming training, in early 1968, from IBM Corp Karachi, Pakistan. Two years later, in 1970, he came to the United States to pursue MS degree, from West Coast University Los Angeles, California. Simultaneously, while pursuing education, he started his professional carrier, as a Systems Representative with Honeywell Inc., a major computer manufacturer, where he remained employed for the next ten years. After Honeywell, for the next two years he was employed as a Vice President in charge of Information Technology department with a firm related to the Oil & Gas Industry segment based in Houston, Texas. It is during this period in 1981, that the author became interested in study of Sufism as a result of reading a book by Adam Smith titled *Powers of Mind*. The intellectual curiosity about Sufism led him to focus on study of the Qur'an and in turn it inspired the author of this book to design a computerized system for online access to the

Qur'anic text, with Arabic-English Lexicon, concordance, dictionary, various translations and related informational databases. This project for Computerized Qur'anic system introduced the author to a group of Sufis living at Bayt-ud-Din in Blanco (near San Antonio), Texas some of whom also had a similar project in mind. This convergence of interest led the author to move to San Antonio, for a period of over fifteen months, to study the Qur'an and to work on the computerized Qur'anic project.

The Bayt-ud-Din Sufi community was guided by a revered teacher Shaykh Fadhlalla Haeri, whose enlightening discourses on the Qur'an, which were a regular feature of daily life, inspired the author to dive further into study of the Divine Book. Over the next twelve years the author actively pursued development of the computerized Qur'anic database. Even today, completion of this project remains a special interest of the author.

Starting with 2004, for the next eight years the author lived in Los Angeles, California, where he often attended Friday prayers at IMAN

(Iranian Muslims Association of North America). At IMAN the pre-prayer sermon was frequently delivered by Dr. Abdullah Gilani, a surgeon by profession. The focus of all of his sermons was exclusively the Qur'an and Dr. Gilani stressed on a non-sectarian approach to Islam always.

Realizing the importance of the revealed message to all humankind, back In 1992, the author had funded launch of a semester long course titled "Introduction to the Qur'an" at the prestigious Rice University of Houston, Texas. This course was taught by Dr. Mehdi Abedi and was received extremely well by the student body.

In June 2008, the author participated, as a presenter, in the first ever Noor Knowledge Conference held in Medina, Saudi Arabia. His presentation was titled *"Keys to Scientific Knowledge in the Qur'an"*. As an example, the presentation referred to some items listed in the Qur'anic text, further research about which could lead to enhancement of human knowledge and new discoveries spanning diverse fields such as about biosciences and information technology. A reference to this presentation here is being made to illustrate that through an inquisitive approach to study of the Qur'an mankind will forever continue to discover hidden secrets about the universal phenomenon and the laws of nature.

> *"There are worse crimes than burning books. One of them is not reading them."*
>
> Multiple Sources